Unselfishness

Unselfishness

The Role of the
Vicarious Affects
in Moral Philosophy
and Social Theory

Nicholas Rescher

University of Pittsburgh Press

Library of Congress Cataloging in Publication Data

Rescher, Nicholas.
    Unselfishness: the role of the vicarious affects
in moral philosophy and social theory.

    Bibliography: p. 115
    Includes index.
    1. Altruism. 2. Ethics. 3. Social ethics.
4. Utilitarianism. I. Title.
BJ1474.R47   171'.8   75-9123
ISBN 0-8229-3308-X

For R. M. Hare
In cordial friendship

Contents

Preface

੬ Few books have been written under more diversified circumstances. Parts were composed in the peace and quiet of my study in Pittsburgh, parts at an altitude of several miles during numerous flights between points in the U.S.A. and Canada, parts in the cloistered library of an Oxford college, parts amid the bustle of medical routine during a period of hospitalization, parts in a scattering of hotel rooms. I trust this circumstantial diversity of its production has not too greatly disturbed the unity of thought and argument.

The central aim of the book is to expound a case for the significance and fundamentality of moral considerations. I want to argue—against a vast host of economists, game theorists, and decision theorists—that one should *not* take the view that rationality conflicts with morality and hold that being moral demands departures from being rational. And I wish to contend against a vast host of philosophers and social theorists that morality is *not* simply a product of intelligent selfishness, of self-interested rationality in an unfamiliar guise.

The virtually universal practice of present-day social scientists working in such fields as economics, game theory, decision theory, and the theory of social interaction is to construe the concept of rationality in terms of self-interest, and to regard conduct that is not self-interested—and perhaps even altruistic—as anomalous and outside the sphere of effective rationalization. Contemporary moral philosophers and social theorists, on the other hand, all too generally adopt a stance that is not dismissive but reductive: they commonly view altruistic behavior as warrantable obliquely by the agent's remote or covert interests and actually in need of such a legitimation in ultimately self-interested terms (and so only *seemingly* possessed of intrinsic worth). Both of these influential views seem to me at bottom untenable—for reasons I shall set out in the ensuing pages.

Morality, I wish to maintain, has an autonomous legitimacy that demands to be dealt with on its own grounds; it is neither at odds with rationality nor amenable to a reduction to prudential considerations. Above all, I wish to defend the position of the older moralists that the worth of altruism is intrinsic rather than reducible to utilitarian maneuverings. But I propose to support these theses not at the level of abstract general principle but by way of an examination of detailed aspects of the workings of unselfishness in theory and practice.

I want to express my thanks to Thomas C. Vinci for helping me polish parts of my draft and to Annette Baier for enabling me to profit from her detailed comments and criticisms. Ernest Sosa also was kind enough to read my manuscript and offer some useful suggestions. I am grateful to the American Council of Learned Societies for a grant-in-aid for support of my research visit in Oxford during the summer of 1973, when the final chapters of the book were drafted and various parts of its earlier argument refined.

I have presented this material in lectures on two occasions, at the University of Western Ontario during the Winter Term of 1973 and at Oxford University during the Trinity Term of 1974. The resulting discussions have helped me smooth out some rough spots in the exposition, and I am grateful to those concerned.

Finally, I wish to express my gratitude to Corpus Christi College for its kindness in providing me an academic foothold in Oxford during the periods I spent there in connection with this project.

NICHOLAS RESCHER

Pittsburgh
Fall, 1974

Unselfishness

1

⌘ The Vicarious Affects and the Modalities of Unselfishness

Sympathy as a "Moral Sentiment"

This study belongs to the wider genus of what Adam Smith called "the theory of moral sentiments."[1] Specifically, its aim is to explore from a philosophical point of view the significant place that must be accorded—within the framework of a workable account of social interactions and a satisfactory moral theory—to the operation of unselfishly sympathetic affections among people. Thus our present concern is not with the complex phenomenology of the moral sentiments in general, but specifically with the one that Adam Smith called "sympathy" and to which he gave the central place in his discussion, describing it in the following terms:

How selfish soever man may be supposed, there are evidently some principles in his nature, which interest him in the fortune of others, and render their happiness necessary to him, though he derives nothing from it, except the pleasure of seeing it. Of this kind is pity or compassion, the emotion which we feel for the misery of others, when we either see it, or are made to conceive it in a very lively manner. That we often derive sorrow from the sorrow of others, is a matter of fact too obvious to require any instances to prove it; for this sentiment, like all the other original passions of human nature, is by no means confined to the virtuous and humane, though they perhaps may feel it with the most exquisite sensibility. The greatest ruffian,

1. In his book of that title. See footnote 2.

3

the most hardened violator of the laws of society, is not altogether without it.[2]

The reason for focusing on this particular "moral sentiment" of sympathy is not that it is the be-all and end-all: admittedly it is only one among many. But the fact remains that it does have considerable importance at the theoretical level, an importance made all the more emphatic by its systematic downgrading by economists since Adam Smith and by its studied neglect throughout most of modern social theorizing. The sympathetic sentiments have been made the focal point of this book not just because of their intrinsic value but because they provide a touchstone, as it were, by which the weaknesses of some parts of recent social philosophizing and theorizing can be brought to light.

The phenomena of sympathy, embracing altruistic and helping behavior, have been studied extensively be psychologists and indeed also by biologists in various animals, especially the higher primates. This study has produced a considerable body of empirical information, much of which is of considerable interest. Nevertheless, this material plays no role in the present discussion. There are two interrelated reasons for this. The first is that the present discussion proceeds on so high a level of generality that specific empirical details have little or no bearing. The second is our concern with the ethical side of the issue, and the empirical relationships—however interesting in their own right—have only a remote and tenuous relation to the evaluative issues that are our primary concern, since these evaluative issues turn on very gross structural considerations pertaining to sympathy, rather than on the finer detail of its operative phenomenology.

Vicarious Affects and Moral Distance (Participatory Kinship)

It is normal, natural, and by and large to be welcomed that a man should participate in the joys and sorrows of his fellows.[3]

2. Adam Smith, *The Theory of Moral Sentiments* (London, 1759), pt. I, sec. I, chap. 1.

3. It being notorious that philosophers are never unanimous on any question, it will come as no surprise that at least one school of moral philosophers does not welcome such participation. The Stoics, who enjoined apathetic indifference

Through positive and negative empathy we are able to enter into the fortunes of others and to share vicariously in developments affecting the welfare and the happiness of those about us. Our own satisfactions and dissatisfactions are thus in substantial measure composed of reactions not to developments that affect us directly and personally, but to our indirect and vicarious participation in the welfare and happiness of other people.

These *vicarious affects* (as I call them) take two principal forms—one positive and one negative—to which we shall give names that fit, if not perfectly, at least reasonably well:

(1) *Sympathy* (communion = *Mitgefühl*): deriving satisfaction (pleasure, enjoyment) from other people's satisfaction and dissatisfaction (displeasure, chagrin) from their dissatisfaction

(2) *Antipathy* (alienation = *Entfremdung*, and typically *envy*): deriving satisfaction from other people's dissatisfaction (that is, *Schadenfreude*, malice) and dissatisfaction from their satisfaction[4]

These are patently the major ways in which people, being constituted as they are, can partake in the joys and sorrows and the goods and evils that the vicissitudes of life bring to their fellow men.

As the old moralists insisted, satisfaction (pleasure, happiness, contentment, etc.) is peculiar in representing a mode of giving without giving up: a man's pleasures (or discontents) can give others pleasure (or discontentment) without thereby being themselves diminished. This capacity to encompass an aspect (positive or negative) of the fate of others is among the characteristics that set man apart from the rest of the animal kingdom—and whose increasingly extensive historical development on the

---

in all matters of human feeling, specifically included the sympathetic feelings in this injunction. "When you see a person weeping in sorrow," says Epictetus, then, "so far as words go, do not be unwilling to show him sympathy, and even if it happens so, to lament with him. But take care that you do not lament internally also." For present purposes, however, we may view the Stoics as the exception that proves the rule.

4. Sympathy and antipathy in this sense might be contrasted with *empathy*, that is, as deriving pleasure or displeasure from something that gives another pleasure or displeasure, but *only* because it does so.

positive side in the course of human history constitutes part of the civilizing process of a widening concern of men for one another.

Though the vicarious affects have recently fallen into unmerited neglect, in former days many philosophers and moralists assigned them a central role in ethical theory. Schopenhauer, for example, in his book *On the Basis of Morality*[5] recognized three fundamental motives as the prime movers of human conduct, to wit, *egoism* (aimed at one's own welfare), *malice* (aimed at the illfare of others), and *sympathy* (aimed at the welfare of others). The philosopher who has discussed the phenomenology of these affects in greatest detail is Spinoza, and Book III of his *Ethics* is devoted to a discussion of them that proceeds at an impressive level of psychological sophistication.[6]

Is sympathy innate or learned? The answer is not a straightforward yes or no, but complex. Studies of children (and of animals also) suggest that while some few modes of sympathy-reaction (for example, to pain-behavior accompanying manifest physical damage or bleeding) may be instinctive, for the most part the vicarious affects represent acquired reactions.[7] Like virtually all forms of moral judgment and action, the vicarious affects are largely learned modes of motivation.

A key aspect of the vicarious affects relates to their rational or motivational *modus operandi:* they function in the order of reasons rather than in the causal order. What is at issue is not just a matter of being pleased or displeased *when* someone enjoys or suffers—for example, by a peculiar blood transfusion or by being somehow cross-connected with that person by wires. The crucial factor is being happy *at* another's happiness by way of *motivation,* being *pleased for* him, valuing someone's good fortune *just because it is his.*

This factor of motivation is crucial. The determinative consideration with respect to benevolence, altruism, etc., is not just *that* a person is concerned for the well-being of others but *why* he is so—namely *because their welfare is at issue.* A person's

---

5. Trans. A. B. Ballock (London, 1903).

6. There is substantial theoretical and empirical literature on the vicarious affects, which is surveyed in the Bibliography.

7. See the Bibliography for the relevant literature.

values become the pivotal consideration here. The vicarious affects come into operation when someone internalizes the welfare (or illfare) of another by way of prizing it on the basis of the relationship that subsists between them—a relationship that may be as tenuous as mere common humanity.

There will, of course, be extreme circumstances under which the principle "every man for himself" may reasonably come to prevail and where a situation of *sauve qui peut* chaos blocks virtually all avenues of mutual involvement that people may have with one another. But our concern is not with such depressively *in extremis* conditions or their euphoric contraries, but with the ordinary situation of *l'homme moyen social:* the social motivations of ordinary people in ordinary circumstances.

The vicarious affects are strikingly associated with interpersonal attitudes in the spectrum ranging from liking or even loving on the positive side to disliking or even hating on the negative. They correlate with and indeed may be taken as prime indicators of the degree of friendliness or antagonism between people. As this perspective makes transparently clear, what is at issue here is quite obviously a matter of degree.

The vicarious affects thus represent the prime expression of what might be called the affective "distance" between people in point of their affinity or disaffinity, that is, the closeness of social and psychic linkage that subsists between them—as man and wife, brother and sister, friends, colleagues, co-workers, or the like. This points toward what might be characterized as affective *affinity groups,* adumbrated by such proverbial dicta as "the friend of a friend is my friend, and the friend of an enemy my enemy."[8] Also, there is no reason of principle why the welfare interests of past or future generations cannot be encompassed within the operative range of the vicarious affects. Just as one can internalize the welfare-interests of distant contemporary strangers (think, for example, of the English slavery abolitionists of the early nineteenth century), so one can also encompass those of our predecessors and our successors. Specifically, there is no good reason why one cannot *and should not* respond by way of affective response to the welfare prospects of future generations. (This shows, incidentally, that an affective

8. Cf. Spinoza, *Ethics*, bk. III, *passim.*

stance can be operative at an aggregative level, without requiring the entry of determinate, identifiable individuals upon the stage of recognition.)

The central facet of the vicarious affects is that when they come in the door, *impartiality* flies out the window. The vicarious affects generate a differential approach in the treatment of other people, underwriting a difference in concern in a man's approach to the welfare-interests of his own parents and to those of other people (to take just one example). Of course, a small handful of philosophers and theologians have repeatedly advocated a strictly universal and impartial benevolence.[9] But neither human nature nor, in the final analysis, ethical theory (as we shall argue) will warrant such a rejection of person-differentiating approaches in interaction situations.

Conscientious professionals, like doctors, teachers, lawyers, trustees, etc., certainly bear the interests of their clients in mind and act for their welfare in a benevolent way. But this need not—and doubtless for reasons of "professional detachment" should not—call the positive vicarious affects into operation. The competent doctor, for example, is no doubt pleased when his patient fares better, but his is presumably a matter of generic satisfaction at a job well done and not the product of his affective participation in the well-being of his patient; indeed, he deliberately does not permit himself "to become personally involved." The conscientious professional, does not connect his own welfare-interests with those of his clients (save insofar as the general rendering of competent professional services is needed to preserve his professional repute).

9. One interesting example is the elder Henry James, father of Henry and William, who wrote as follows in a letter to son Henry: "Your long sickness, and Alice's, and now Willy's have been an immense discipline for me, in gradually teaching me to universalize my sympathies. . . . But when I gained a truer perception of the case, and saw . . . that I should perhaps scarcely suffer at all, if other people's children alone were in question, and mine were left to enjoy their wonted health and peace, I grew ashamed of myself, and consented to ask for the amelioration of their lot only as part of the common lot. This is what we want, and this alone, for God's eternal sabbath in our nature, the reconciliation of the individual and the universal interest in humanity" (R. B. Perry, *The Thought and Character of William James*, Briefer Version [Cambridge, Mass., 1935], pp. 3-4).

THE VICARIOUS AFFECTS AND UNSELFISHNESS

A recognition of the vicarious affects serves to clarify the workings of the family of concepts associated with the ideas of altruism, unselfishness, and a disinterested concern for the welfare of others. For it is clear that the happiness (utility) we derive from the happiness (utility) of others can be disinterested as well as interested. And even when it is interested, it may be either *unselfishly* interested (when, by virtue of some suitable relationship, we legitimately "form an interest" in their welfare) or *selfishly* interested (say through the recognition that, when happy, they are more likely to act to make us happy too, so that we become happy through anticipation).

Specifically, it is appropriate to distinguish several distinct cases:

(1) The *other-regarding* (rather than *purely self-interested*) person is one who cares for the welfare of others (in the sense of prizing or valuing it), and for whom the latter's interests and well-being are matters of genuine concern.

(2) A person is *interestedly other-regarding* if his regard for the welfare of others is motivated by the (essentially selfish) consideration that his own welfare is so bound up with theirs that the promotion of their welfare is indirectly a means for promoting his own. He is *benevolent* if he is *disinterestedly other-regarding;* that is, if the welfare of others is of positive concern to him in *its own right,* without ulterior motives, and thus regardless of any reference to possible repercussions for his own welfare.

(3) A person is *altruistic* (rather than *egoistic*) if he gives such weight to the welfare of others that he is prepared in principle to subordinate his own welfare to that of others, setting his own welfare aside in the interest of theirs in certain circumstances.

The most delicate distinction here is that between, on the one hand, the interested but unselfish concern for the condition of a person in whom one *has formed an interest* and, on the other hand, a strictly disinterested concern. In the former case (that of "interested but unselfish"), one's care for the other's welfare (or pleasure) proceeds with an eye to one's own overall welfare-interests as well, so that another's welfare (or happiness) is at least in part a determining factor for one's own. In the latter case, one cares for the other's welfare solely for its own sake, without reference to repercussions for oneself and one's own interests. The difference between rendering unselfish help to a perfect stranger and rendering it to someone in whom one has somehow come to form an interest illustrates the distinction. Of course, there will be borderline cases; for example, can the person who regularly supports organizations that aid the blind eventually be said to have formed an interest in the blind?

Be this as it may, one can proceed on the indicated basis to elaborate an exposition of the various modalities of unselfishness along the lines of the table "The Modalities of Unselfishness."

An example may help to clarify these rather abstract distinctions. Consider a population of five persons, A to E, and suppose that one of them, A, can so act as to bring about any of the following distributions of utility:

	No. 1	No. 2	No. 3	No. 4
A	5	4	4	4
B	4	5	4	5
C	4	4	4	5
D	4	4	4	4
E	4	4	5	4

If A is totally selfish, he will automatically choose distribution No. 1 in preference to all others, since he personally fares better than in any other case. If A is self-indifferent, he will be indifferent between distributions Nos. 1, 2, and 3, for he equates the welfare of the person who is so fortunate as to attain 5 units on distribution No. 1—namely, *himself*—with the welfare of any of the individuals who would be similarly positioned on any of the other distributions. Finally, A would be self-sacrificing in preferring distribution No. 4 to distribution No. 1 since he would, in this case, subordinate his own good to that of others (since in distribution No. 4, unlike No. 1, two persons are 5-unit beneficiaries).

Within the framework of this classificatory scheme we may characterize action motivated by the *positive* vicarious affects as benevolent as well as altruistic, though not necessarily disin-

The Modalities of Unselfishness

	Character Trait	Type of Motivation	Contrary Opposite
1.	Other-regarding (in its positive sense)	Prizes the welfare of others (possibly for "ulterior motives")	Other-discounting (or purely self-interested)
2.	Benevolent (disinterestedly other-regarding)	Prizes the welfare of others in its own right, without "ulterior motives"*	Malevolent
3.	Altruistic†	Gives such weight to the welfare of others that their interests can in principle override his own within the framework of his own moral calculations	Egoistic
4.	Disinterested	Disregards repercussions for his own welfare (leaves himself out of the moral calculation)	Totally selfish
5.	Self-indifferent	Puts his own welfare on a plane with that of others; i.e., manages to be *impartial* between his own welfare-interests and those of others	Either *self-sacrificing* or *self-aggrandizing*, depending on the direction of differentiation (see no. 6)
6.	Self-sacrificing	Systematically discounts (deemphasizes) his own welfare vis-à-vis that of others (sets theirs above his)	Self-aggrandizing

*Herbert Spencer defined the trait that, following the phrenologists, he called *benevolence* as getting pleasure by giving others pleasure. But this takes an unduly activistic view of benevolence, which can also take the passive, spectatorial form of deriving pleasure from mere contemplation of the pleasure of others, regardless of the issue of *by whom* this is given.

†The term "altruism" is a relatively recent coinage. It was introduced by Auguste Comte to designate devotion to the welfare of others as a principle of action.

terested or self-sacrificing. (The positive vicarious affects are altruistic because they provide for the subordination and/or the discounting of one's purely self-oriented interests in some cases.) Of course, if one were to construe the concept of *self*-interest in a wider sense than the self-serving construction commonly given it, one could say that the vicarious affects are never "disinterested" because of their role in determining just what a person's interests (in this enhanced sense) actually are. But a vicarious affect as such—in the absence of further detail—is indeterminate in point of *self-interest*, in the ordinary sense of the term.

The person who is actuated by positive vicarious affects toward others—who gives to *their* first-order welfare some weight in constituting *his own* in the second order—certainly need not be said to be wholly selfless or unselfish. But in insisting on the reality of the vicarious affects, one need not deny the possibility of such total selflessness or utter unselfishness or the like. It is only maintained that *one* significant form of unselfishness takes the route of a *partial* appropriation (internalization) of the welfare situation of others.

Accordingly, the concept of a person's *interests* will have to be construed in a rather more complex way than usual, for due distinctions must be introduced when a man's interests are in part *constituted* with reference to the welfare-concerns of others. We must now differentiate his *narrow self-interest*, oriented toward his own personal, egocentric condition, and his *wider self-interest*, which now operates in an enlarged sense and also takes due account of the welfare condition of others toward whom he stands in a relation of affective kinship.

Once the vicarious affects are brought upon the scene, somebody might be tempted to argue as follows:

> The vicarious affects put our concern for others in a distinctly unflattering light. For when someone who has such an affect acts ostensibly to benefit its subject, he may really be acting selfishly for the sake of benefits accruing obliquely to himself. He may prize another's good just because it has become a means to his own—that is, as a mediate mode of furthering his personal benefit.

In this way, the vicarious affects might be viewed exclusively from the point of *self-interested* other-regardingness.

But this is nonsensical. One can only deny the fundamentally unselfish aspect of the vicarious affects—the positive ones, at any rate—by wholly ignoring the role of motivation and the workings of human psychology. The crucial issue is posed by the question of the motive force behind the internalization of another's welfare. As things go in the world, this internalization is in general not just a matter of conditioning, or some such automatic process, but is produced by the motivational force of a *concern* for certain others, an actual engagement in their well-being or welfare. We must be careful not to put the cart before the horse: a person who is positively disposed to another does not in general welcome what is beneficial to this other because this other's happiness somehow conduces to his own; rather, the case is reversed—his own augmentation of happiness is a strictly incidental reactive product of that of the other.

In normal circumstances, at any rate, one welcomes another's benefits just *because* they are his benefits, and not because they somehow benefit oneself through the mechanism of internalization as an oblique way of furthering one's own good. It would be not only unusual but even perverse to welcome the happiness of others simply as a mediate means toward one's own. The vicarious affects—in their standard mode of operation—envisage the welfare of another not only as being a determinative consideration of a person's welfare but as representing a significant motivating consideration. It is not just that *X* is made happier/unhappier *by* increases/decreases in *Y*'s welfare, but that he is made so *because* of this in the reason-oriented rather than the cause-oriented sense of the term.

This fact that the vicarious affects operate not just in a causal manner but by way of *motivation* renders the positive vicarious affects genuinely unselfish in their standard *modus operandi*. Only if we abstract from the psychological realities entirely, ignoring how people come to have vicarious affects in the first place, can we fail to perceive this inherently unselfish aspect. Accordingly, an unselfish act does not become less unselfish because one gets satisfaction from its performance (any more than a morally right act becomes less creditable because its performance gives one satisfaction—Kant to the contrary notwithstanding).

ETHICAL LEGITIMACY OF THE VICARIOUS AFFECTS AND MORAL JUSTIFICATION OF DIFFERENTIAL TREATMENT

There can be no question about the *de facto* reality of the vicarious affects at the empirical or phenomenological level. Admittedly, people do have important immediate, selfish, and self-oriented interests. But that is certainly not the end of the matter. Through the process of internalization, the interests of others do figure, in a highly selective way, as part of our own in an extended sense. To be sure, this happens in a highly differential manner: our own children are closer to us than our neighbors' children, our intimate friends closer than casual acquaintances, our neighbors closer than "people at large." But, nonetheless, all our fellow men figure somewhere along the line (as indeed animals may, especially pets).[10] The reality of this general phenomenon is a matter of familiar and unquestionable fact.

Moreover, the vicarious affects have—at any rate on the positive, sympathetic side—a solid foundation of rational warrant in moral philosophy, a warrant that operates through the closeness of the relationship between the parties involved and is embedded not only in formalized contracts but in the social contract of the customs and mores of the group. A husband's interests are bound up with those of his wife in ways that transcend the selfish factor of mutual advantage; the same applies with parents and their children. Such relationships link the interests of persons into networks of intimacy and remoteness that make a mockery at the level of individual deliberation of the claims of the utilitarian dictum that "each is to count for one, no one for more than one" as a precept for everyday human interactions. And this circumstance is a matter not just of how things are but of how they should be in terms of the moral proprieties of the matter.

---

10. William James wrote that one "can never hope to *sympathize* in a genuine sense of the word with [elephants and tigers]. And the want of sympathy is not as in the case of some deformed or loathsome human life, for their being is admirable; so admirable that one yearns to be in some way its sharer, partner, or accomplice" (R. B. Perry, *The Thought and Character of William James*, Briefer Version [Cambridge, Mass., 1935], p. 224). James seems to be mistaken here in exaggerating the extent to which the feelings at issue in "sympathy" must be capable of reciprocation. But he is no doubt right that sympathy has its limits—one cannot sympathize with a statue!

To *disregard* the interests of others is to be not merely *immoral* but *inhuman*. And to insist on treating all alike—in the spirit of the utilitarian dictum—is almost as bad: not inhuman but heartless, not praiseworthy but morally obtuse (save, of course, in the legislator, judge, government official, or other person whose duty points, *ex officio*, indifferently to all alike).[11]

The positive (that is, sympathetic) vicarious affects in fact represent worthy, morally commendable attitudes: sympathy, fellow-feeling, human solidarity, and the like. There is no question that they merit recognition and approval from an ethical point of view. And the moral bearing of the vicarious affects cuts deep. To help our brother in need (say) from a sense of duty pure and simple, but without any feeling of sympathy, without some degree of affective involvement in his ill fortune, is (*pace* Kant) rather discreditable than otherwise. Internalization of the weal of our fellows (duly differential in bearing) is, in appropriate circumstances, not only morally justified (permissible) but even mandatory.[12]

To be a *person* is correlative with recognizing the personhood of others and with standing in morally appropriate sorts of interrelationships with them. To gainsay the legitimacy of revising our immediately self-regarding interests from an other-regarding point of view—denying the legitimacy of reinterpreting our "self-interest" in a larger sense that also embraces the interests of others in proportion to the closeness of their connection with us—is a policy that has little to recommend it. Certainly this step does *not* deserve having it urged on its behalf that it is the *morally* defensible thing to do in terms of a workable ethical theory.

The moral legitimacy of the vicarious affects has important ramifications. At bottom they represent motivational factors that

11. In the case of professional functionaries (rather than public officials) there will also, of course, be cases where one expects "professional detachment" to be maintained through appropriate measures for the suppression of personal involvement.

12. I would not, however, go so far as some writers who cast sympathy in the role of a *precondition* for moral action (for example, Philip Mercer, *Sympathy and Ethics* [Oxford, 1972], p. 134). Not *all* moral obligations—so it seems to me—can demand an element of sympathy in their motivating force, if only for the simple reason that sympathy itself, is, in certain circumstances, morally obligatory. (We shall return in the next section to the issue of how *feelings* can be matters of obligation.)

are closely bound up with the emotions, and consequent upon the fact of affinity between persons. But this emotional aspect is only the beginning of the matter, not its end. The fact that the mechanism of vicarious involvement ultimately has a foundation of legitimation in moral theory means that what is at issue here is not merely emotional but has a rational dimension as well: it is not just a part of the phenomenology of man's emotional life but enjoys a suitable basis of rational warrant relating to their role in shaping an appropriate setting for the conduct of human affairs.

But one important qualification is necessary. From the standpoint of ethical legitimation, the positive vicarious affects have an altogether different ethical footing than the negative. For the negative (that is, antipathetic) vicarious affects in fact represent unworthy, morally negative attitudes: hostility, malice, envy, jealousy, *Schadenfreude*, and the like. From an ethical point of view they merit nonrecognition and dismissal as reprehensible. Thus all is well and good as regards A's accession of utility (increase in satisfactions), derived from B's *gains* therein; this utility-increment of A's deserves to be taken into positive account. But if A's increase in satisfactions derives from B's *losses* therein—if A's condition of satisfaction is *augmented* by B's losses and sufferings—this deserves dismissal in the reckoning (and, similarly, if A's dissatisfaction derives from B's gains). In short, only the results of the sympathetic vicarious affects merit recognition as valid from the moral point of view.

To be sure, one cannot deny that, on occasion, envy and its congeners may militate toward a socially benign end. There is, after all, but a thin line between a sense of justice that leads one to demand one's rights and outright displeasure in another's unmerited better fortune. However, this is beside the point of our present concern with the ethical coloration of the negative affects. For ends do not justify means, and ethically reprehensible arrangements are not transmuted into positivity by the fortuitous fact that they conduce, in certain circumstances, to positive results.

From this perspective, the crucial question is not just whether people are more or less well off in point of utility (or more or less happy, for that matter) but also *how* they get that way; that is, whether by morally salubrious or morally deleterious means. From the moral point of view, the positive (sympathetic) and the negative (antipathetic) vicarious affects thus stand on altogether different footings.

But the key fact remains that once *any* of the vicarious affects (specifically the positive ones) are seen as legitimate and worthy to be recognized and reckoned within the ethical appraisal of situations involving the interests of people, we also validate thereby the ethical justification for the differential treatment by one individual of his fellows. For insofar as a person is justified in internalizing (in part) *A*'s gains and losses rather than *B*'s, he may also be justified in opting for a situation in which it is *A*'s condition that is improved rather than *B*'s. The ethical legitimacy of certain vicarious affects will, in suitable circumstances, produce the moral justification for a differential treatment of people. Once the ethical legitimacy of the (positive) vicarious affects is admitted, a differential approach to people is rationalized; it no longer stands at the reprehensible level of a mere prejudice.

Of course, our sole concern throughout this section has been with the delimited claim that the vicarious affects—or at any rate some of them—have a status of moral legitimation and validity. We have not yet attempted to deal with *what* that status is. And we have not—to be quite specific on this point—maintained that the (positive) vicarious affects are *self*-warranting, and that their legitimacy is altogether intrinsic, neither needing nor permitting validation in terms of other more ultimate factors of moral theory. Quite to the contrary. It is our view that their validity rests on other, extrinsic considerations. But this important issue cannot be pursued in this initiating chapter; it will receive the attention it demands in chapter 6.

APPENDIX: SIDGWICK ON BENEVOLENCE

No philosophical writer has, to my knowledge, treated the range of issues revolving about benevolence with greater theoretical sophistication and keener sensitivity to the issues involved than Henry Sidgwick.[13] And yet even his treatment is an odd mixture of clearheaded insight and obscuring wrongheadedness.

13. Henry Sidgwick, *The Methods of Ethics*, 7th ed. (London, 1907), bk. III, chap. 4, "Benevolence," pp. 238–63.

Most philosophers treat benevolence only as that universally applicable moral sentiment whose maxim is "we ought to love all our fellow men"—a universalized *philanthropy* (in the root sense of that term). The great merit of Sidgwick's treatment is that he clearly sees benevolence as extending beyond this universalized sense, recognizing that "the special function of Benevolence begins where Justice ends; and it is rather with this special function that we are concerned in considering claims to affection, and to kind services normally prompted by affection" (p. 242).

Accordingly, Sidgwick is aware of the requirement that an adequate moral theory must be prepared to accommodate those special and person-discriminating "duties that arise out of relations where affection normally exists, and where it ought to be cultivated, and where its absence is deplored if not blamed" (p. 243). Through this stress on affection Sidgwick recognizes the existence and legitimacy of the differential force of a man's affective involvements. Sidgwick proceeds to furnish an inventory of the various sorts of human relationships that produce circumstances under which such a duty "to cultivate affection so far as is possible to do so" comes into operation:

They seem to range themselves under four heads. There are (1) duties arising out of comparatively permanent relationships not voluntarily chosen, such as Kindred and in most cases Citizenship and Neighbourhood: (2) those of similar relationships voluntarily contracted, such as Friendship: (3) those that spring from special services received, or Duties of Gratitude: and (4) those that seem due to special need, or Duties of Pity. [p. 248]

The only criticism one can make of this sensible listing is that while it envisages only relationsips that are "comparatively permanent," one might also expect the positive affects to come into operation (at least to some modest degree) on the basis of transitory relationships, as are operative in the case of fellow passengers, messmates, classmates, etc.

Yet another merit of Sidgwick's treatment is implicit in this passage. Some writers might quite mistakenly maintain that *feelings* cannot be a matter of moral concern, since they cannot be a matter of duty because "a person can't help how he feels." Sidgwick rightly stresses that this will not do:

I agree that it cannot be a strict duty to feel an emotion, so far as it is not directly within the power of the Will to produce it at any given time. . . . [But nevertheless] it will be a duty to cultivate the affection so far as it is possible to do so. . . . At any rate, it would seem to be a duty generally . . . to cultivate kind affections toward those whom we ought to benefit; not only by doing kind actions, but by placing ourselves under any natural influences which experience shows to have a tendency to produce affection. [p. 239]

This recognition that persons can, at least to some extent, exercise effective control over their feelings is certainly a point of strength in Sidgwick's treatment of these issues.

However, from our perspective, the main shortcoming of Sidgwick's position also appears clearly from the preceding discussion. His approach to benevolence proceeds wholly in terms of claims and duties. His concern as moralist is limited to clarifying the "*claims* to affection" which one person may have upon another in view of the special relationships that subsist between them, and the correlative *duties* that result from such claims:

Common Sense, however, seems rather to regard it as immediately certain without any such deduction that we owe special dues of kindness to those who stand in special relations to us. The question then is, on what principles, when any case of doubt or apparent conflict of duties arises, we are to determine the nature and extent of the special claims to affection and kind services which arise out of these particular relations of human beings. [p. 242]

Such approach gives his discussion an unduly legalistic cast, and it leads to a damaging neglect of the aspect of internalization and the fundamentally unselfish quasi-self-interest we have in the well-being of those with whom we are affectively involved.

This emphasis on the "*duties* of affection" led Sidgwick down a primrose path in dealing with the moral role and the implications of benevolence. For it is clear that, quite apart from the issue of "duties to have affection," which can be treated in a reasonably exact way, there is the issue of "duties that derive from affective relationships," and that this duty-oriented aspect of the matter is a shady area, not readily amenable to the considerations of abstract general principle with which moral philosophers traditionally deal. This issue of tidiness in the operation of general principles is something that Sidgwick treats at length:

It is sometimes given as a distinction between Justice and Benevolence, that the services which Justice prescribes can be claimed as a

right by their recipient, while Benevolence is essentially uncon-
strained: but we certainly think (*e.g.*) that parents have a right to filial
affection and to the services that naturally spring from it. It is further
said that the duties of Affection are essentially indefinite, while those
we classify under the head of Justice are precisely defined: and no
doubt this is partly true. We not only find it hard to say exactly how
much a son owes his parents, but we are even reluctant to investigate
this: we do not think that he ought to ask for a precise measure of his
duty, in order that he may do just so much and no more; while a great
part of Justice consists in the observance of stated agreements and
precise rules. At the same time it is difficult to maintain this distinction as a ground of classification; for the duties of Affection are admittedly liable to come into competition with each other, and with
other duties; and when this apparent conflict of duties occurs, we
manifestly need as precise a definition as possible of the conflicting
obligations, in order to make a reasonable choice among the alternatives of conduct presented to us. [pp. 242-43]

His search for exactness in the specification, for the weight
and interrelationship of the "*duties* of affection," led Sidgwick
to regard the claims of benevolence as in the final analysis inherent
in justice, since he believes that all duties and obligations must
ultimately inhere in more fundamental principles—namely, those
of justice—on the basis of which various conflicts of duty can
be adjudicated:

In conclusion, then, we must admit that while we find a number of
broad and more or less indefinite rules unhesitatingly laid down by
Common Sense in this department of duty, it is difficult or impossible
to extract from them, so far as they are commonly accepted, any
clear and precise principles for determining the extent of the duty
in any case. . . . In reply it may perhaps be contended that if we are
seeking exactness in the determination of duty, we have begun by ex-
amining the wrong notion: that, in short, we ought to have examined
Justice rather than Benevolence. It may be admitted that we cannot
find as much exactness as we sometimes practically need, but merely
considering the common conceptions of the duties to which men are
prompted by natural affections; but it may still be maintained that we
shall at any rate find such exactness adequately provided for under
the head of Justice. [pp. 262-63]

This standpoint that the obligations of affection can be rationalized in terms of the principles of justice creates substantial
difficulties. For the principles of justice are—as Sidgwick quite
properly holds—effectively *universal* in scope and applicability:

they specify a degree of generality and impartiality that seemingly conflicts with the differentiating impact of affective relationships. A destructive tension arises in Sidgwick's discussion between the impartiality of justice and the discriminative bearing of affective relationships. The problem of validating person-differentiating acts on the basis of person-indifferent principles poses serious—and in my view ultimately fatal—difficulties for Sidgwick's treatment of benevolence. We shall have occasion to consider the ramifications of this problem in chapter 5. But it is now time to terminate this historical digression and return to the vicarious affects.

2

✍ The Workings of the Vicarious Affects

PARTICIPATORY TRANSFER

Clearly, when one person participates in the good and bad fortunes of another through an affective internalization of this other's condition in point of welfare, the extent to which he does so is a matter of degree—of more or less. In this connection one might well think of a *participatory transfer rate* (p.t.r.), indicative of the relative extent to which one participates vicariously in another's fortunes. This obviously is a complex matter that hinges on many considerations, but two of these will clearly be of primary weight:

(1) "Affiliation": the closeness of kinship between the persons involved in terms of their "affective distance"
(2) "Receptiveness" or "vulnerability": a given person's intrinsic capacity for internalizing the welfare of others by way of positive or negative reaction[1]

The mechanism of such a rate of participatory transfer or appropriation obviously demands a closer scrutiny. Thus far we have taken account only of the qualitative aspect of this phenomenon, but its quantitative aspect must also be considered.

To put the matter in technical jargon, a person's overall utility-condition can be viewed as consisting of two components: the *first-order utility* (as we shall call it) of what affects one

---

1. This factor of vulnerability raises the prospect of amplification: a piece of good fortune might give a man modest pleasure, but his augmented pleasure might please his wife or sister a great deal.

22

directly and personally, and also (by no means negligibly) the *second-order utility* that devolves from the vicarious affects—the goods and evils that befall one not immediately, but only through one's participatory sharing in the conditions and circumstances of others. Accordingly, given any allocation or distribution of "utility" (welfare, well-being, happiness, etc.) to various people, the utility-status of any individual can be regarded from two perspectives:

(1) His *first-order* utility-status, determined on what might be termed a *prima facie* basis, that is, without any reference to his affective involvement with the fate of others

(2) His *second-order* utility-status, incorporating into his utility-condition a part of the condition of others, duly internalized through a vicarious participation in the welfare of others

In distinguishing between first- and second-order utility, we recognize the feedback effects, inherently operative in all allocations of "utility," which inhere in the circumstance that any distribution of utilities itself affects the utilities actually secured by the parties because of their affective interrelationships. This internally complex structure of utility, as having both a first-order and a second-order component, is lost sight of when one goes no further than to conceive of the issue in monolithically uniform terms such as the satisfaction of desires. For the crucial distinction must be drawn *internally* to this range, namely, between what one desires for oneself (strictly self-oriented desires) and what one desires for others and *on their account,* rather than on one's own (other-oriented desires).

The upshot is that utilities cannot be looked on as simply the *inputs* to such distributions or redistributions but will, to some extent, also function in the role of outputs. Since the concept of second-order utility takes account of a very real phenomenon—the vicarious affects—it represents a more comprehensive and, thus, a more realistic basis for the appraisal of the circumstances of people in point of their utility-condition. It envisages a sort of "participatory transfer payment" made by some individuals to others in their affective proximity (to borrow a bit of economists' jargon). It is obvious that when the vicarious affects come into operation, the *net* effect of a fixed *gross* addition (or decrease) in utility will be highly variable, depending on the specific pattern of the distribution in terms of just who gets what.

THE NATURE OF AFFECTIVE DIFFUSION

Once it is recognized that people participate by way of internalization in the well-being of others—their joys and sorrows, welfare and illfare—it becomes clear that this launches a repetitive process that can in principle go on without end. For we embark upon a series of the "I'm glad you're glad I'm glad you're glad" type that can go on *ad indefinitum*. This iteration seemingly threatens the viability of the ideas at issue with a vitiating regress, and does indeed produce conceptual disaster if we think of vicarious participation in the *sum total* of another's utility understood in the second-order sense. For, clearly, if it were a matter of internalizing the absolute amount of another's utility, the whole process would become unworkable. Suppose that A and B each has 10 units of "utility" and that they react sympathetically to each other's utility-status at, say, a positive appropriation rate of 10 percent. Then A would take over 1 unit of B's utility, raising his own to 11. And B will take over 1.1 unit of A's, raising his to 11.1. And A would take over 10 percent of this, raising his own to 12.1. And so on—with the result that the utility stock of each would grow *ad infinitum*, there being no way of bringing the cumulative process to a halt at any given stage.

Thus if one is to conceptualize the workings of the vicarious affects in the manner proposed above—as a *rate* of appropriation or transfer (the p.t.r.)—one must be careful to save the idea from self-destruction, by insisting that only first-order utility is involved in the transfer indicated by such a rate, and that the rate itself is designed to reflect *the whole iterative process* of reactions to reactions, insofar as such a feedback effect comes into play. The p.t.r. is to represent *the all-comprising upshot that results "when everything is said and done,"* rather than indicate some intermediate stage that leaves room for yet further stages of calculation. We want to cut off the threat of a degeneratively explosive cycle of increasingly piling joy on joy—or a degeneratively implosive one of increasingly piling misery on misery.

This conception of the workings of a p.t.r. thus serves to

avoid the seeming unrealism of supposing a flat percentage rate applied to first-order utility, thus postulating a transfer made in a one-shot manner. To feel distress if others starve, but not if they watch their children starve, is admittedly a psychological impossibility—and one that is certainly *not* supposed by our approach. Our p.t.r. is intended to represent the result of the whole iterative transfer process. (This complexity surely does not render the whole idea unworkable: in most practical cases, the mixture of shared misery and pleasure, and the practical limits to reflexive complexity, will presumably help to stabilize the quantity involved at some definite level.)

Moreover, it seems plausible that participatory transfer operates in such a way that it is not a fraction (or percentage) of the *total amount* of utility that is taken over and internalized, but only the *change in amount* from a certain "initial situation" fixed by the conditions of the case. Nor is it a psychologically unrealistic supposition to think that the vicarious affects behave in this *incremental* way, and that our participation in the welfare of others relates not to its absolute amount but to its changes (increases or decreases) from the norm of "what we have come to expect" for these persons in terms of the point of departure defined by the circumstances in which we find them when they come upon the stage of consideration for us.[2] Alternative policies are available for determining this background "initial utility-situation," which constitutes the *norm* by departures from which the participatory transfer of the vicarious affects comes into operation. We might posit that

(1) the norm is a "hypothetically neutral" *starting position of zero utility,* so that the difference between the initial and the norm-relative utility status is obliterated;

(2) the norm is the average of the initial utility distribution for *all* individuals (or for all within a certain category to which the individual at issue belongs);[3]

(3) the norm is the *de facto* condition in point of utility in

2. This is admittedly mere armchair psychology. It would be interesting to have some empirical data.

3. Or one could readjust this average with a view to equity in distribution. Cf. the concept of an *effective average* developed in N. Rescher, *Distributive Justice* (New York, 1966).

which one finds the person when one initially encounters him.

In presenting examples it is convenient sometimes to take the one and sometimes the other line in this matter of a basic norm, the first approach being generally preferable on grounds of convenience in calculation.

How could a person's p.t.r. *vis-à-vis* others possibly be determined in practice? The key issue, presumably, is the extent to which one is prepared to sacrifice one's own (first-order) welfare-interests to those of others because one prizes it. In the first approximation (admittedly only a very imperfect one), this "preparedness to sacrifice" could be assessed in terms of actual expenditures of resources (money, time, effort). Of course, the voluntary aspect is crucial here: the support of public-welfare programs through taxation does not necessarily reflect affective involvement.

From the angle of operational measurement, probably the simplest effective test of the workings of the positive vicarious affects is in terms of a goal-expenditure analysis that proceeds by reckoning the amount expended for the benefit of others and for which there is no direct or oblique return (for example, the personal resources expended on the education of children once the "they'll support us in our old age" principle becomes inoperative; or, on the national level, by reckoning expenditures on "unproductive" foreign aid and on "unproductive" domestic groups, such as the very aged or the chronically ill). In this sense, the vicarious affects, and in particular the positive ones, are not preoccupied with mere *justice,* but with something exceeding it—not with what is "the just due" of the objects of one's participatory interest, but with their good fortune. Affection transcends the minimalistic demands of justice.

The Method of Calculation

To get a clearer view of the workings of the vicarious affects under the sort of conditions set out above, a bit of formal calculation is useful. Consider a population of individuals A_1, A_2, A_3, ..., A_n whose utility-shares are a_1, a_2, a_3, ..., a_n respectively. Moreover, let p_{ij} = the participatory transfer rate of the i-th individual (A_i) with respect to the j-th individual

(A_j); thus p_{ij} is the *percentage* of A_j's utility that is internalized by A_i.

Accordingly, we have it that t_{ij}, the *amount* of the utility that the i-th individual (A_i) derives from the j-th individual (A_j), may be calculated as follows:

$$t_{ij} = (a_j - N) \times p_{ij}$$

where N is the "background norm" against which the utility-condition of the individual A_i is appraised. We may (for example) suppose, for the sake of simplicity, that N is simply the average utility-condition of people-in-general:

$$N = \frac{1}{n} \sum_i a_i$$

(with n = the total number of individuals at issue).

Now the overall sum total of the second-order utility that a given individual derives from all of the rest will be calculated as follows:

$$u_i = a_i + \sum_{\text{all } j \neq i} t_{ij} = a_i + \sum_{\text{all } j \neq i} (a_j - N) \times p_{ij}.$$

This formula spells out in detail how, on the basis of the principles set out in the preceding section, we propose to handle the workings of the vicarious affects.

In keeping with this line of thought, it is proposed throughout the present discussion to accommodate the vicarious affects in the manner of the following example. Let it be assumed that we are confronted with a micro-society of eight persons whose utility-statuses in terms of gains or losses in relation to "the norm" are as follows:

A_1	+20	A_5	+20
A_2	+10	A_6	+10
A_3	−10	A_7	−10
A_4	−10	A_8	−10

Suppose, further, that this society splits into the two camps

A_1 to A_4 and A_5 to A_8, within which people are positively disposed toward one another at a p.t.r. of +20 percent, but which are mutually antagonistic in such a way that across the boundary a p.t.r. of −10 percent is operative. Then it will eventuate that utilities are distributed as in the tabulation on the following page. This example illustrates the general process by which we propose to take the vicarious affects into account.

The complaint can doubtless be lodged—and with much justice—that this percentage-transfer treatment of the vicarious affects is too simplistic. But this objection need not trouble us overmuch. The obvious reply is that clearly it is better to be in a position to take account of the vicarious affects in an imperfect or oversimplified way than to accept the shortcomings of leaving them wholly out of account by ignoring them altogether. And, in any case, our concern is with the general phenomenon of the vicarious affects rather than with the specific mechanics of their operational detail. The processes of calculation are deployed simply to obtain concrete illustrations of basic phenomena. None of the theoretical points at issue is crucially dependent on the specific method of quantitative treatment, in the sense of becoming "unstuck" if some other plausible process of calculation were introduced instead.

The Vicarious Affects and Strategies of Choice

Consider a person (A) who must choose between alternatives regarding the utility-status of a group (A, B, C), himself included. Suppose the choice to be as follows (as regards the first-order utilities):

Alternative I			Alternative II	
A	+ 5		A	+ 5
B	+10		B	− 5
C	− 5		C	+10

Suppose A were impartial between B and C. Then clearly he would also be indifferent to the two alternatives. On the other hand, if A favored B (and therefore alternative I), we would certainly expect him (A) to have a positive vicarious disposition toward B, with the result that the choice in effect

The Operation of the Vicarious Affects

Individual	Utility Derived From								Resultant Utility
	A_1	A_2	A_3	A_4	A_5	A_6	A_7	A_8	Σ
A_1	+20	+ .2	− .2	− .2	− .2	− .1	+ .1	+ .1	+19.7
A_2	+ .4	+10	− .2	− .2	− .2	− .1	+ .1	+ .1	+ 9.9
A_3	+ .4	+ .2	−10	− .2	− .2	− .1	+ .1	+ .1	− 9.7
A_4	+ .4	+ .2	− .2	−10	− .2	− .1	+ .1	+ .1	− 9.7
A_5	− .2	− .1	+ .1	+ .1	+20	+ .2	− .2	− .2	+19.7
A_6	− .2	− .1	+ .1	+ .1	+ .4	+10	− .2	− .2	+ 9.9
A_7	− .2	− .1	+ .1	+ .1	+ .4	+ .2	− .2	− .2	− 9.7
A_8	− .2	− .1	+ .1	+ .1	+ .4	+ .2	− .2	−10	− 9.7

looks somewhat as follows from A's standpoint (postulating—for him [alone]—a p.t.r. of +20 percent toward B):

	I			II
A	+ 7		A	+ 4
B	+10		B	− 5
C	− 5		C	+10

As one would expect, the two alternatives no longer have an effectively indifferent look from A's point of view.

These considerations point to an important lesson, namely, that a person's strategy of choice among alternatives that effect redistributions of utility (prudential safety-first, altruistic self-denial, etc.) should be reflected in the vicarious affects attributed to him. At the level of abstract theory, a discrepancy can of course arise. One could in theory transform a given redistribution of first-order utilities into second-order utilities on one set of principles, and then suppose a variant principle of selection among alternatives that proceeds on a different and discordant basis. But in practice this discrepancy must be avoided. Any reasonable application of the machinery at issue must envisage a homogeneity of consistency and coordination between the postulated vicarious affects on the one hand and, on the other, the assumedly operative principles of choice among alternatives.

Thus, for example, we would not wish on the one hand to impute to A a strategy of selection that is wholly self-interested, and on the other hand to credit him at the affective level with a positive disposition toward B, say at a p.t.r. of +10 percent. For then the initial situation

	I			II
A	+10		A	+9.95
B	+ 5		B	+6

would be transformed to

	I′			II′
A	+10 + 0.50 = +10.50		A	+9.95 + 0.6 = +10.55
B	+5		B	+6

and so *A* would—given the dominance considerations at the level of second-order utilities—be led to the second alternative, notwithstanding the strictly self-interested *modus operandi* we have postualted for him. In applying the machinery developed here, one should maintain an overall consistency of approach.

It is possible to consider some variations of this approach, which I shall sketch only briefly, without much development. Thus one might let the p.t.r.'s at issue be adjusted in a *variable* way, relative to the given utility-distribution itself, by fixing the p.t.r. with reference to this distribution. For instance, people might *readjust* their vicarious participation in line with the utility-shares of the beneficiaries of a distribution, say by internalizing larger gains at a discount. Thus let us assume a microsociety of five persons, *A* to *E*, each of whom is positively inclined to the others at a basic p.t.r. of 10 percent, but in such a way as to discount *larger-than-average benefits* in proportion to their excess over the average, that is, by the factor

$$\frac{\text{Average benefit}}{\text{Larger-than-average benefit at issue}}.$$

Consider now the case of a first-order utility-distribution:

A	+ 0
B	+ 0
C	+100
D	+ 40
E	+ 10

Here the average benefit is +30, and two individuals, namely, *C* and *D*, exceed it. Then—on the assumptions we have introduced—the others would value a given person's benefit at 10 percent, save in the case of the "fat cats" *C* and *D*, with respect to whom the p.t.r. would now be reduced to

C	$10\% \times 30/100 = 3\%$
D	$10\% \times 30/40\ = 7\tfrac{1}{2}\%$

Accordingly, the second-order utility distribution would be

A	7
B	7
C	104
D	44
E	16

and not, as would be the case without the discounting under consideration,

A	15
B	15
C	105
D	51
E	24

Such a relative discounting of gains by the "fortunate" (or, viewed from the other side, relative accentuation of gains by the "unfortunate") would be one way of superimposing phenomena like jealousy or pity upon the mechanisms under consideration. Our subsequent considerations, however, will not make such refinements.

The crucial thing at this stage is that we have shaped a (hopefully) workable account of the nature of the vicarious affects and have devised at least a rough-and-ready method for dealing with their mode of operation. This done, it is time to consider some contexts in which they can be applied to profitable effect.

3

ॐ Rationality and the "Prisoner's Dilemma"

THE PARADOXICAL ASPECT OF THE PRISONER'S DILEMMA

The term "prisoner's dilemma," attributed to the Princeton mathematician A. W. Tucker, is taken from the anecdote originally used to illustrate the special sort of game situation at issue. Two prisoners, held incommunicado, are charged with being accomplices in the commission of a crime. For conviction, the testimony of each is needed to incriminate the other. If each confesses, the result is mutual incrimination, and both will divide the penalty of twenty years' imprisonment. If only one turns state's evidence and confesses, thereby incriminating the other (who maintains silence), the whole penalty will fall on this hapless unfortunate. But if both maintain silence and neither confesses, both will suffer a much-diminished penalty (say two years' imprisonment). The prisoners face the problem of whether to take a chance on confession or to opt for the possible benefit of silence, accompanied by an even greater risk.

We may represent the situation of two-person interaction in which the prisoner's dilemma arises by the game matrix:

X \\ Y	C	$\bar{C}$
C	$-10/-10$	$0/-20$
$\bar{C}$	$-20/0$	$-2/-2$

The numbers in this so-called pay-off matrix represent gains or losses (that is, negative payoffs) for the two participants (in this case years of imprisonment), with a tabulated entry x/y

33

representing the results x for X and y for Y, respectively, under the different combinations of choices between C for "confess" and $\bar{C}$ for "don't confess." And we are, of course, to envisage an equality of conditions in terms of life expectancy, incarcerative ennui, etc., so that an effective parity is preserved in the significance of these figures for the two parties involved. The dilemma arises because *if* one of the prisoners does what group solidarity demands as proper (namely, $\bar{C}$), *then* he runs the great risk that his partner will instead follow the course of safety (namely, C), with the result that he alone is sunk; but if *both* prisoners do the safe thing (namely, C), they arrive at a result $(-10/-10)$ that is far worse for their common interest than the outcome $(-2/-2)$ reached when both act more trustingly. The dilemma for each prisoner is whether to rely on the discretion of his accomplice.[1]

Students of social theory almost invariably regard this prisoner's dilemma situation as presenting a paradoxical circumstance in social interaction, but in fact this example becomes *paradoxical* only when we have been dragooned into assuming the stance of the theory of games itself. Just how does the game theorist envisage the problem-solving task of participants in a situation of choice under uncertainty in situations of conflict? For the game theorist, the resolution for a participant lies in the identification of a choice-alternative upon whose implementation the participant *fares no worse than otherwise, regardless of what his opponents do*. Thus in the prisoner's dilemma example, if X opts for C, and then

(1) If Y opts for C, X gets -10 (in contrast with -20 for his $\bar{C}$)

(2) If Y opts for $\bar{C}$, X gets 0 (in contrast with -2 for his $\bar{C}$)

Thus C represents the game theorists' logical answer to X's choice-problem in terms of a prudential strategy of self-interested

---

1. For a detailed discussion of the "prisoner's dilemma" see Morton D. David, *Game Theory* (New York, 1970), pp. 92–103. See also A. Rapoport and A. M. Chammah, *Prisoner's Dilemma: A Study in Conflict and Cooperation* (Ann Arbor, 1965), and Anatol Rapoport, "Escape from Paradox," *American Scientist*, 217 (1967): 50–56.

"safety-first": C dominates $\bar{C}$ in putting X into a better position regardless of Y's choice. It seems to put X into the best defensive position, come what may.

And, of course, because of the total symmetry of the case, the game-theory approach also leads Y inexorably to C. Accordingly, the prospect of realizing the attracitve result $-2/-2$ is altogether lost. Because of dominace considerations, the mutually unhappy result C/C qualifies, on the game-theoretic approach, as the appropriate resolution to the dilemma in which the prisoners find themselves. By taking what the game theorist insists upon as the proper step—the very quintessence of prudential rationality—the participants fail to reach their mutually preferred result.

Now the crucial thing to notice is that there is in fact nothing whatever *paradoxical* about this circumstance. It shows merely that the realization of a generally advantageous result may require the running of individual risks, and that the pursuit of other-disinterested prudence may produce a situation in which the general interest of the community is impaired. For these lessons we did not need to await modern game theory; the moralists of classical antiquity told us as much many years ago.

Thus there is nothing actually paradoxical in this example for anyone who is not minded from the outset to regard the game theorists' recommendations of "playing it safe" as representing the best policy to guide our social-interaction choices. For the game theorist takes safety and prudence as his guiding stars, and that *this* strategy does not necessarily produce universally optimal results is close to truistic (and moreover is encapsulated in the old dictum that "faint heart ne'er won fair lady").

ALTERNATIVES TO PRUDENCE

Certainly very different types of "solution" to conflict interaction situations are perfectly possible and represent approaches that differ very fundamentally from the game theorists' strictly prudential, play-it-safe strategy. Two alternatives in particular demand recognition:

(i) The *negotiative* "solution": that at which the participants would arrive in a negotiation conducted rationally (and with full candor on both sides), with each party shrewdly in pursuit of his own self-interest. (In the prisoner's dilemma this would be the mutual adoption of $\bar{C}$ with the result $-2/-2$.)

(ii) The *general-interest* "solution": that which would be selected by a rational, impartial arbiter concerned to advance the interests of group members in a person-indifferent way and to bring about a situation that is optimal from "the social point of view" of the parties involved, taken as a group. (In the prisoner's dilemma case this would again lead to the outcome $-2/-2$.)

This second mode of "solution" would not in general be identical with (i) above, because a participant could enjoy a threat-posture that would enable him to force a negotiation toward his own advantage, at variance with the indifferently appraised interests of the group as a whole. To see the sharp difference between the two modes of "solution" of a conflict-of-interest situation, consider the following case of a variant "game-situation":

$X \diagdown^{\displaystyle Y}$	y_1	y_2
x_1	5/10	10/0
x_2	9/−100	9/−100

Here the *negotiative* "solution" is $x_1 y_2$ (10/0). It is arrived at as follows: X points out to Y that unless Y does as he, X, wants him to do, namely to select y_2, X will simply select x_2, with very little cost (regardless of Y's action) to X himself, compared with what he would otherwise realize, but with disastrous consequences for Y. Thus X's negotiative position is such that he can force the outcome $x_1 y_2$ (10/0), and can thus assure that he, X, will fare better in the outcome than he could under any other alternative. In the negotiative approach to resolution the parties are free to exploit this sort of threat-potential. (Of course, in this negotiative approach the ground rules of the game-theoretic approach are altered, and communication between the parties must be presupposed.)

Finally, the *general-interest* "solution" is $x_1 y_1$ (5/10). An altogether impartial arbiter (of the type familiar in philosophical discussions of the "ideal observer" theory of moral appraisal) would simply note that the various possible outcomes are as follows:

	The Party Who Fares Best Obtains	The Party Who Fares Second-Best Obtains
$x_1 y_1$	$+10$	$+ 5$
$x_1 y_2$	$+10$	0
$x_2 y_1$	$+ 9$	-100
$x_2 y_2$	$+ 9$	-100

This display makes it transparently clear that an impartial arbitrator would opt for $x_1 y_1$. On the other hand, the game-theoretic analysis produces the result that no definite solution is to be obtained. To be sure, from Y's position, one is led to select y_1, since regardless of what X does, one fares better here (or at least no worse) than one would do otherwise. But there is no comparably "prudent" course open to X.

It might, of course, be objected that these varying modes of "solution" are irrelevant to the prisoner's dilemma situation because the prisoners are held incommunicado, so that negotiation or arbitration is, by hypothesis, infeasible. But this objection is not decisive, for there is nothing to prevent the prisoners from proceeding *as though* they were negotiating or subjecting themselves to the decision of an arbitrator. There is, in short, nothing to exclude the sort of *tacit* negotiation and/or arbitration that would result if the prisoners assumed the appropriate hypothetical stance. The point is that there is nothing internal to the circumstances of the problem-situation itself that constrains the prisoners to proceed on the basis of self-interestedly prudential considerations alone, to the exclusion of a duly enlarged social point of view.

In the context of the prisoner's dilemma problem, the important fact emerges that there are modes of "solution" to these conflict-of-interest situations that differ radically from the safety-first rationale of the orthodox game-theoretic approach. The implications of this fact warrant closer scrutiny; in particular, the conception of the "general-interest" solution of impartial arbitration will be studied in detail in the next chapter.

Some Lessons of the Prisoner's Dilemma

From the vantage point of these distinctions between various types of "solution" to a social interaction situation involving a conflict of interest, one can discern a confusion that is rife in the economic and philosophical literature of this sphere: the failure to maintain a sufficiently sharp distinction between prudence and rationality.

Virtually all writers on the economic aspect of the subject unblushingly identify *rationality* with what is, in effect, simply *self-interested prudence.* Without further ado, they assume the stance that any reference to the interests of others would be discounted altogether by the rational man. Accordingly, the prisoner's dilemma has for them a markedly paradoxical aspect. Construing rationality wholly in terms of self-oriented prudence, they see the prisoner's dilemma as illustrating a surprising conflict between rationality and self-interested advantage. The literature of game theory is accordingly replete with claims to the following effect: "In the game called Prisoner's Dilemma, the rational choice of strategy by both players leads to an outcome which is worse, for both, than if they had chosen their strategies 'irrationally.' "[2]

But this just is not so. It is not *rationality,* but *the prudentially safety-first-minded pursuit of personal advantage,* that the example shows to be at variance with social optimality and the good of all.

The widely current interpretation in terms of *rationality* begs two key questions:

(1) Whether rationality demands the prudential, safety-first approach (rather than, say, the strategy of a shrewdly calculated risk)[3]

2. A. Rapoport and A. M. Chammah, *Prisoner's Dilemma: A Study in Conflict and Cooperation* (Ann Arbor, 1965), p. 13. Or, as Rapoport puts it in another place: "The paradox is that if both players make the rational choice, . . . both lose" ("Escape from Paradox," *Scientific American,* 217 [1967]: 51).

"Of course, it is slightly uncomfortable that two so-called irrational players will both fare much better than two so-called rational ones" (R. D. Luce and H. Raiffa, *Games and Decisions* [New York, 1957], p. 96).

Writers on this point of game theory sometimes speak of "rational" or *so-called rational* behavior, putting us on warning that something is amiss, but never go so far as to recognize that they would be best advised simply to give up speaking of *rationality* in this connection.

3. "The theory of games is a valuable tool in making more determinate our understanding of rational self-interest. For the 'solutions' it provides to conflict situations are solutions for rationally self-interested men—instructions which they may follow in order to maximize their expected utilities, or in other words, their expected well-being" (Luce and Raiffa, *Games and Decisions,* p. 20).

(2) Whether rationality demands a cultivation of personal advantage to the exclusion of the interests of others

Clearly, both of these points are eminently debatable. Having already aspersed the game theorists' construction of rationality in terms of safety-first prudentialism, I shall confine my remarks to the second point, that rationality is strictly self-regarding.

On this head, it would seem that the vicarious affects teach an important lesson. People undeniably have important immediate, selfish, and self-oriented interests. But that is certainly not the end of the matter. The interests of others can also be made to figure through internalization as part of our own. No doubt this happens in a highly differential way: our own children are "closer" to us than our neighbors' children, our neighbors closer than "people at large," but nonetheless all our fellow men figure somewhere along the line. That is how it is and how it should be—and there is nothing whatever irrational or nonrational about it. To *disregard* the interests of others is not rational but inhuman. And there is nothing *irrational* about construing our self-interest in a larger sense that also takes the interests of others into account, albeit in a highly differential way. To deny the legitimacy of revising our immediately self-regarding utilities from an other-regarding point of view is a step that has little to recommend it. Certainly this step does *not* deserve to have it urged on its behalf that it is the *rational* (let alone the *moral*) thing to do.

There is, in fact, no substantial reason for taking the view that the prisoner's dilemma—or any other example—shows that *rationality* is incompatible with heeding the interests of others. (That *selfishness* is incompatible is no doubt true but altogether trite.) Moral philosophers must fight to the knife against the economists' chronic tendency to equate rationality with the prudential pursuit of self-interested advantage.

It is a travesty upon this concept to construe *rationality* in terms of prudential self-advantage, for there is nothing in any way inherently unreasonable or irrational about a concern for others. Indeed, there is no adequate reason for calling a man unreasonable if his actions militate against his own interest—for

---

This is quite wrong. The theory of games deals not in *expectations* but in *safeguards*.

there is no earthly reason why he cannot have perfectly legitimate values that transcend his interests. To be sure, a man will be unreasonable, indeed irrational, if his actions systematically tend to impede his objectives. But there is no adequate ground for holding that his *only* rationally legitimate objectives are of the selfish or self-interested sort.

The true moral of the prisoner's dilemma story is quite different from the oft-drawn conclusion that rationality can be at odds with the general good. The prisoner's dilemma brings out the important lesson that there are situations in which following the dictates of prudence does not produce the result that best advances the interests of everyone concerned (specifically including the prudent individual himself). And, in particular, there are situations in which the policy of prudence and risk-minimizing caution is not efficient in the promotion of self-interest. These points, though true enough, will surely be familiar to the point of triteness. They have been the common currency of moral philosopers since classical antiquity.

Looked upon in its proper perspective, the prisoner's dilemma offers the moral philosopher nothing novel. Its shock-effect for students of political economy inheres solely in their ill-advised approach to *rationality* in terms of a prudential pursuit of selfish advantage. We are thus brought again to a recognition of the shortcomings of the concept of "economic man" and the economists' traditional conception of rationality in terms of the efficient pursuit of prudential self-interest.[4] When it is objected that this view quite unrealistically renders each man a self-centered island, one might counter that there is no reason why "self-interest" should not be construed in an enlightened and widened sense to include the interests of others, through the operation of the vicarious affects. This objection is certainly well taken, but it will not serve as a defense that hard-line economists would care to use. For them, the usefulness of the underlying economic model of human nature was seen to derive from the very simplicity of its concept of a person's interests.

As long as interests are construed in other-ignoring, wholly self-oriented terms, the procedures needed to take them into

---

4. This is reflected throughout the older literature in economics as well as in the most recent literature of the theory of games.

account remain relatively simple, but this simplicity and work-ability are lost when one introduces other-referring complications into the issue of how the "interests" of a person are in fact constituted. And—as we shall see below—once one embarks upon a division of interests into the *strictu sensu* self-serving and a wider and other-embracing sense, one introduces moral complexities into the calculation that impede this model of rationality from serving the sorts of purposes generally envisaged for it.

Is one to construe a person's interest in strictly self-oriented, selfish terms (in which case the move from self-interest to benevolence and/or morality is clearly blocked at the theoretical level)? Or are we to construe it as including, also as an integral component, his other-interested, vicarious involvements with other people (in which case the move from interest to other-concern is greatly faciltated)? Once such distinctions and divisions are allowed to enter into the determination of interests—as it seems they in fact must—the specification of rationality in terms of interest becomes infeasible. For then the thesis that rationality revolves about interests shatters at once on the question of legitimation, of the discrimination between true or legitimate interests (for example, health) versus false or illegitimate interests (such as those represented by greed, power madness, lechery, etc.). And here rationality cannot be determined by interests (the basic game is now simply given up!), because interest itself must be weighed in the scales of rationality. Once this issue of the *rationality of ends* is admitted by recognizing that different sorts of interests can stand on a different footing than legitimacy, one renders unattainable the prospect of a unidirectional determination of rationality with reference to interests.

THE PERILS OF NAIVE BENEVOLENCE: THE SAINT'S DILEMMA

The preceding section has argued that rationality should not be construed as tantamount to self-oriented prudence. But in all fairness I wish now to concede to the traditional economists' view of the matter that a morality of disinterested other-concern certainly need not inevitably be rational either.

D. P. Gauthier has recently maintained that "if all men are moral, all will do better than if all are prudent. But any one man will always do better if he is prudent than if he is moral.

There is no real paradox in supposing that morality is advantageous, even though it requires the performance of disadvantageous acts."[5] But such a view that universal moral behavior is conducive to selfish advantage—however true it might be under certain suitable contingent conditions—is not true as a matter of principle. It can be rendered incorrect by the workings of something like an "After you, Alphonse—No, after you, Gaston" phenomenon. There is, after all, no difficulty in showing that social-interaction situations can unquestionably arise in which the parties are led to a mutually suboptimal result by being *too mindful* of the welfare of others.

It is well worth noting that, while the prisoner's dilemma brings home the disadvantages of prudentially safety-first-minded self-interest, analogous examples can be devised to illustrate the shortcomings of a naive (and prudentially articulated) benevolence or "selflessness."

Observe that in the original prisoner's dilemma example, IF each participant "puts the interest of his fellow ahead of his own," and acts in an utterly self-indifferent, selflessly benevolent way, caring *only* for the welfare of his fellows, THEN the original payoff matrix is in effect transformed—by the simple process of a switching of affective roles (and thus inverting the payoffs)—into

X \ Y	C	$\bar{C}$
C	$-10/-10$	$-20/0$
$\bar{C}$	$0/-20$	$-2/-2$

The game-theoretic "solution" is now $\bar{C}/\bar{C}$ with the payoff $-2/-2$, producing the outcome that in this case the prudential mode of (game-theoretic, safety-first) resolution happily leads to the result that best realizes "the general interest." In this particular case, the selfless course of "putting ourselves in the other fellow's shoes" indeed produces the socially optimal result.

But the significant fact remains that this is by no means the case in general. In fact, universal benevolence (implemented

---

5. D. P. Gauthier, "Morality and Advantage," in *idem*, ed., *Morality and Rational Self-Interest* (Englewood Cliffs, N.J., 1970), p. 175.

in this prudential manner) can virtually produce universal disaster. Thus consider the situation

X \ Y	y_1	y_2
x_1	$-100/-100$	$-101/+6$
x_2	$+6/-101$	$+5/+5$

The "selflessly benevolent" transform of this (obtained simply by interchanging the "payoffs" for X and Y) is

X \ Y	y_1	y_2
x_1	$-100/-100$	$+6/-101$
x_2	$-101/+6$	$+5/+5$

The game-theoretic "solution" here is x_1y_1, for if X selects x_1, he will never fare worse than otherwise, regardless of what Y does; and the analogous circumstance holds for Y. (This reflects, with respect to the initial situation, the fact that if X opts for x_1 in this initial situation, Y will never fare worse than otherwise, and analogously for Y.) Thus in cases of *this* sort, prudential selflessness produces the result that is, among all possibilities, the one most damaging to the general interest.

This fact too, that such naive altruism can engender unfortunate results, has long been recognized by moralists and novelists alike. Indeed, it is not uncommon to find ethical theorists castigating naive selflessness in such terms as those of Moritz Schlick:

The unrestricted development of such [altruistic] inclinations . . . can certainly not lead to the valuable, and will not, in fact, be considered moral. To respect every desire of one's neighbor, to give in to every sympathetic impulse results, finally, neither in the highest measure of joy for the individual himself, nor indeed for the others; in such a case one no longer speaks of kindness, but of *weakness*.[6]

Naive and unthinking benevolence can unquestionably prove personally unsatisfying and morally counterproductive.

6. Moritz Schlick, *Problems of Ethics*, trans. D. Rynin (New York, 1939), pp. 202-3.

THE POSITIVE AFFECTS AND THE "SOCIAL POINT OF VIEW"

Against the background of such derogatory observations about naive benevolence, it should be said that the tendency of the positive affects is ordinarily such as to reinforce the general welfare and the social point of view. Accordingly, it is useful to reconsider problems of the prisoner's dilemma type from the vantage point of the vicarious affects.

When the vicarious affects are taken into proper account in a social-interaction situation of the game-theoretic sort, the result is a transformation of the matrix of *prima facie* or first-order utilities. It is not necessarily the procedure of calculation that differs; rather, the very numbers with which we calculate come to be altered.

Consider the prisoner's dilemma once more. The initial payoff matrix runs

X \ Y	C	$\bar{C}$
C	$-10/-10$	$0/-20$
$\bar{C}$	$-20/0$	$-2/-2$

But suppose that both parties are altruistic to at least *some* extent: that each is prepared to assume "the social point of view" and attach at least *some* value to the interests of the other. Specifically, let us suppose that both participants in this social-interaction situation incline positively toward each other at a participatory transfer rate of, say, 20 percent. The result would then be

X \ Y	C	$\bar{C}$
C	$-12/-12$	$-4/-20$
$\bar{C}$	$-20/-4$	$-2.4/-2.4$

Note that, given this transformed grouping of "payoffs," the old game-theoretic "solution" of $X_C Y_C$ is now dissolved. But it is important to note that we have, of course, reached *inside* the original payoff matrix to manipulate the numbers that are at issue, and so *altered* the very "rules of the games."[7]

Moreover, if each participant is *very* altruistic, taking over the utility-result for his partner at full value (with a p.t.r. of +100 percent), we obtain

X \ Y	C	$\bar{C}$
C	$-20/-20$	$-20/-20$
$\bar{C}$	$-20/-20$	$-4/-4$

This is the situation "it hurts me as much as it hurts you." Now in this case the game-theoretic solution becomes $X_{\bar{C}}Y_{\bar{C}}$. And we see that in a sufficiently altruistic group we reach the result that the prisoner's dilemma becomes such that the strictly prudential resolution comes to be socially optimal as well as personally advantageous.

The crucial point, then, is that the very nature of the "problem" posed by a prisoner's dilemma situation is transformed for the parties involved—and comes to look like a very different sort of issue—once the prisoners are assumed to take an enlarged view of the situation, one that is not wholly self-oriented but also envisages due heed for the welfare of others.

To be sure, someone may at this point object as follows:

> All that your introduction of the vicarious affects manages to achieve is to show that some situations can—given a sufficiently high participatory transfer rate—be *transformed from conflict to nonconflict cases*. Your appeal to the vicarious affects does not really point the way toward any better methods for solving cases of actual conflict.

This objection is good enough as far as it goes, but is too rigoristic in its understanding of what is involved in "solving" a problem of this sort. After all, a transformation that removes a problem in certain cases is, for these cases, as good as a *solution* (for

7. This treatment of the problem is something of an oversimplification, for it treats the affective involvement of the parties in such a way as to consider only the vicarious negativities of the other's imprisonment, without providing for the vicarious positivities of the other's freedom. But this oversimplification is harmless—it facilitates the construction of the example without leading to any errors in more fundamental matters.

all practical purposes, and many theoretical ones as well).

In a world where the (second-order) utility of each sufficiently internalizes the (first-order) utility of his fellows, we can rely much more confidently upon prudential calculations to lead to socially beneficial results. This is something that may well happen. But it need not. For, needless to say, *this* circumstance of the prisoner's dilemma case is not inevitable. It needs little emphasis that cases *can* arise where a duly internalized heed of the interests of others will call for a *sacrifice* in selfish advantage. (Again, it does not require the theory of games to teach us this lesson.)

It is worthwhile to be explicit about one point that emerges from these considerations. With the entry of the vicarious affects, one transforms "raw," first-order utilities into "cooked," other-considering, second-order ones. Now, even given this revision of the basic parameters of calculation in situations of choice or conflict, the question of a strategy of resolution—be it self-interestedly prudential or negotiative or impartially arbitrative—remains unresolved. But one result of the discussion is that the prisoner's dilemma problem can be taken as illustrative of that significant family of cases where internalization at the affective level will produce a socially benign result—and manage to do so even when at the interactive level the strategy of resolution remains strictly prudential.

The crucial point, however, remains that prudential calculation bears an altogether different aspect from the moral point of view when we shape the utility-functions that measure the extent to which something is in a person's own interest with some reference to the interests of others. When we *internalize* the interests of others, the calculations of self-interest will generally lead to results more closely attuned to the general interests of the group. When the interests of others enter sufficiently into the determination of our own interests, the description of a person as prudentially "calculating" loses much of it morally pejorative stigma.

From this standpoint, the question of selfish advantage in the concern for others is left hanging in the air, suspended from the hook of empirical considerations. It now becomes a purely contingent question whether the world is such that the prisoner's dilemma is paradigmatically typical, that is, whether sufficient internalization of the interests of others ultimately pays off in terms of selfish advantage. That a situation of this sort *can* exist is something we well know (and the prisoner's dilemma reminds us of it). Whether the circumstances of our life are such that these situations *predominate,* so that a moral concern for others is not only morally commendable but also represents "the best policy" in terms of selfish advantage, remains an issue for *empirical* investigation. (And, at any rate, we do have a *moral* obligation to produce a life-setting in which other-regarding behavior is self-interestedly beneficial. Not many moralists have stressed this, but it is certainly known to the plain man and manifestly affects his view of the role of law and the morality of punishment.)

ASPECTS OF THE PRISONER'S DILEMMA PROBLEM FROM THE
ANGLE OF INTERNALIZATION

It thus becomes germane to reconsider the prisoner's dilemma perplexity from the vantage point of the vicarious affects and to contemplate the case where each of the parties involved is prepared to internalize the well-being of the other at some positive participatory transfer rate of $r > 0$. We begin with the matrix of *prima facie* payoffs:

X \ Y	y_1	y_2
x_1	$-10/-10$	$0/-20$
x_2	$-20/0$	$-2/-2$

Through the operation of the vicarious affects in the stipulated manner, this comes to be transformed into the following matrix of second-order "payoffs":

X \ Y	y_1	y_2
x_1	$-10 + r(-10)/-10 + r(-10)$	$0 + r(-20)/-20 + r(0)$
x_2	$-20 + r(0)/0 + r(-20)$	$-2 + r(-2)/-2 + r(-2)$

Of course, if we were to have $r = 0$, we would be back with the original prisoner's dilemma case. But as r increases toward $+1$, the situation is altered drastically—as we have seen above.

To have the dilemma-situation arise, it would have to be the case that, as regards X, both

$$(i) \quad -10 + r(-10) \geq -20 + r(0)$$

and also

$$(ii) \quad 0 + r(-20) \geq -2 + r(-2).$$

Now let us focus on the second of these:

$$-20 \, r \geq -2 - 2 \, r$$

$$-18 \, r \geq -2$$

$$-r \geq \frac{-2}{18}$$

$$r < \frac{1}{9}$$

Thus the moment $1/9 < r$ obtains, one of the conditions for reaching a prisoner's dilemma collapses. Of course, this approach to the prisoner's dilemma presupposes a uniform condition of the two parties in point of mutual affective involvement. (In circumstances where this bilateral uniformity is absent, the issue would work itself out rather differently, in ways the reader can readily determine for himself, subject to whatever specific assumptions he cares to introduce.)[8]

This, then, is the prime lesson: the parties were entrapped in the "dilemma" because they did not internalize the welfare of their fellows sufficiently. If they do this, and do so in sufficient degree, they can escape the dilemmatic situation.

---

8. Thus if, for example, X valued Y's condition at a p.t.r. of $+30\%$ while Y valued X's at -30%, we would have

X \ Y	y_1	y_2
x_1	$-13/-7$	$-6/-20$
x_2	$-20/6$	$-2.6/-1.4$

Now Y is lead to y_1 by dominance considerations, but safety-first no longer provides X with decisive guidance.

But at this stage the following objection might be advanced:

This treatment of the issue implies that a prisoner's dilemma situation can be overcome through sympathetic internalization by the parties involved of the welfare of others. But the dilemma might surely arise *after* positive internalization as well as before. Internalization affords no effective solution for the problem if cases of the prisoner's dilemma type can be *created* through the operation of the positive vicarious affects.

To handle this objection, let us begin by asking: What would an initial pre-internalization situation have to be like for the vicarious affects to be so operative that a prisoner's dilemma condition results? Again, let r represent the rate (be it 10 percent or 20 percent or whatever, so long as $0 < r < +1$), at which X and Y internalize one another's good. And let the initial position that is to give rise, after internalization, to the prisoner's dilemma situation of

X $\diagdown$ Y	y_1	y_2
x_1	$-10/-10$	$0/-20$
x_2	$-20/0$	$-2/-2$

now be represented as follows:

X $\diagdown$ Y	y_1	y_2
x_1	x_{11}/y_{11}	x_{12}/y_{12}
x_2	x_{21}/y_{21}	x_{22}/y_{22}

Looking to the top left-hand entry of the matrix, we note that we must have it that

$$x_{11} + ry_{11} = -10$$

and

$$y_{11} + rx_{11} = -10.$$

Solving this pair of linear equations, we arrive at

$$x_{11} = \frac{-10}{r+1}, \quad y_{11} = \frac{-10}{r+1}.$$

And carrying out this process for the entire matrix, we see that the resultant matrix will in fact amount to

X $\diagdown$ Y	y_1	y_2
x_1	$\dfrac{-10}{r+1} \Big/ \dfrac{-10}{r+1}$	$\dfrac{-20r}{r^2-1} \Big/ \dfrac{+20}{r^2-1}$
x_2	$\dfrac{20}{r^2-1} \Big/ \dfrac{-20r}{r^2-1}$	$\dfrac{-2}{r+1} \Big/ \dfrac{-2}{r+1}$

Treating the here omnipresent positive multiplier $1/(r + 1)$ as tantamount simply to a scaling factor, we arrive at the matrix

X $\diagdown$ Y	y_1	y_2
x_1	$-10/-10$	$\dfrac{-20r}{r-1} \Big/ \dfrac{+20}{r-1}$
x_2	$\dfrac{20}{r-1} \Big/ \dfrac{-20r}{r-1}$	$-2/-2$

We thus arrive at the question: How would this matrix lead to a prisoner's dilemma solution at x_1y_1 with payoff $-10/-10$? The answer is that this result would be reached if, and only if, *both* of the following conditions upon r are realized:

$$-10 > \frac{20}{r-1} \qquad\qquad \frac{-20\,r}{r-1} > -2$$
$$-10(r-1) < 20^9 \qquad -20r < -2(r-1)$$
$$-(r-1) < 2 \qquad\qquad -20r < -2\,r+2$$
$$1 - r < 2 \qquad\qquad -18r < +2$$
$$-r < 1 \qquad\qquad -r < \frac{1}{9}$$
$$-1 < r \qquad\qquad -\frac{1}{9} < r$$

9. Note that the inequality is reversed because the multiplier of its two sides $(r - 1)$ is by hypothesis a negative quantity.

The first of these conditions obtains trivially. And the second is also automatic for any positive r. Thus in *every* case of the sort at issue where the (uniform) operation of the positive vicarious affects produces a prisoner's dilemma situation, the *original* situation from which a prisoner's dilemma is to arise after internalization *must itself already represent a prisoner's dilemma.*

The upshot is that the (positive) vicarious affects can never produce a prisoner's dilemma situation where one was not present in the first place. Given that they operate more or less uniformly among the parties involved, they cannot generate the dilemma from an initially unproblematic situation. Thus we need not worry ourselves that the positive vicarious affects could so operate as to *create* a prisoner's dilemma situation that was not there to begin with.

4

～ Conflict Situations and the Social Point of View

THE IDEA OF AN "IMPARTIAL ARBITER'S APPROACH"
TO CONFLICT RESOLUTION

Let us explore in somewhat greater detail the conception of an "arbitrator's solution" to social-interaction problems that manifest a conflict of interests, as mooted in the preceding chapter. We shall again proceed by taking some characteristic cases that can be described simply and with great precision, drawing upon the theory of games.[1]

Consider a very straightforward example. Imagine a social group of just two members, X and Y, and let it be that X and Y can achieve a mutually beneficial result by arriving at any one of five available alternative courses of action. Suppose further that the mutually beneficial result at issue is in fact worth \$100 to X and \$200 to Y, but that the different courses of action involve different costs to X and Y, according to the following schedule:

---

1. Actually, most of the points to be made here can be made with games of a very simple sort: two-person games, albeit not zero-sum games. The formal theory of such non-zero-sum games is still relatively underdeveloped, but this is relatively immaterial for our rather simpleminded purposes. A major contribution is T. C. Schelling, *The Strategy of Conflict* (Cambridge, Mass., 1960). The prime application of game theory to social situations is due to R. B. Braithwaite, *The Theory of Games as a Tool for the Moral Philosopher* (Cambridge, 1955). For a good general account of game theory, with full reference to the contributions importantly relevant to our discussion see R. D. Luce and H. Raiffa, *Games and Decisions* (New York, 1957).

Alternative	Cost to X	Cost to Y
I	$110	$ 30
II	80	50
III	60	100
IV	30	120
V	0	150

This produces the following upshot:

Alternative	Net Benefit to X	Net Benefit to Y
I	−$ 10	+$170
II	+ 20	+ 150
III	+ 40	+ 100
IV	+ 70	+ 80
V	+ 100	+ 50

As part of the conditions of the problem we shall make the usual assumption that the "utility of money" is to be exactly the same for the members of the group (that is, the relative value they place on money is identical and its relative usefulness is the same, so that, for example, X is not so rich that the gain or loss of a few dollars is a matter of indifference for him). Moreover, we have to exclude the prospect of making compensating payoffs "on the side," so that, for example, Y cannot bribe X to adopt alternative I, with a subsequent compensation of $80, producing the (otherwise unavailable) result of $70 for X and $120 for Y. Finally, we must assume an effective condition of parity between the parties in those respects that do not "meet the eye" in the statement of the problem itself (so that, for example, a third-party arbiter would not be tempted to reduce injustices originating elsewhere by an award in the case in hand that cannot be rationalized in terms of the conditions of the case itself).

It is not of concern at present to explore the essentially "political" aspect of the matter, relating primarily to the issue of an arrangement the participants constrain among themselves by *force majeure*. (Such a political power struggle can be highly contingent, involving many issues external to the problem itself; for example, how "tough" the various members are willing and able to be as negotiators.) Rather, our problem is one of determining the "socially desirable" solution, one that a reasonable, benevolent, and impartial spectator would consider "best for everyone concerned"—the sort of solution a friendly and disinterested third party would propose to the parties involved if they came to him as arbitrator. We need not, of course, assume for such an arbitrator any "higher legitimacy" than that inherent in the interests and wishes of the parties themselves, the "best interests of the group." To be sure, his reference to their interests should be in an essentially *retrospective or hypothetical mode:* "*If* they were to accept his recommendation, *the parties themselves* would, if 'reasonable,' be better pleased *on balance* (as to cases) *and in the aggregate* (as to persons) than with any alternative solution."

Exactly what sort of "arbitration" is to be at issue? Here we shall assume—and this assumption is essential to everything that follows—that the arbitrator's dominant motivation is a *strictly impartial benevolence* or, in other words, a *concern for the general good that is wholly indifferent to persons and their circumstances of relative advantage.*

Arbitration, as we envisage it, aims at making a *rational* award, one for which a rational defense on reasonable general principles can be given. The leading considerations operative here are benevolence, impartiality, and moral sagacity. In seeking to implement the social point of view *vis-à-vis* the multiplicity of self-interested parties, it is conceivable that the result may prove at variance with the views of one of the parties to such an extent that he regards it as unacceptable and withdraws from arbitration. We view this prospect with equanimity. Our problem is to spell out the conditions of a reasonable answer for the group as a whole. That people may in fact be unreasonable is undeniable—and beside the point. (Perhaps one could also think in terms of sanctions invoked by the rest of society to enforce such a "reasonable" resolution against the overt wishes of the parties themselves, for example, in judicial arbitration.) At any rate, our concern is with the "rights and wrongs" of the matter, and not its "practical politics." The critical point is that the arbiter is impartial between the parties, benevolent toward them, and judicious in his appraisal of considerations bearing upon their interests.

Given *this* conception of how an impartially benevolent arbitrator is to go about his business, we can see that the example would appear as follows from the standpoint of such an arbiter. He is concerned with a two-member society (the members of which are otherwise equally "deserving" as far as the arbitrator is concerned). He can assure any of the following outcomes for the two members of this society, X and Y:

$$-10/+170; \ +20/+150; \ +40/+100; \ +70/+80; \ +100/+50.$$

From the arbitrator's perspective, it is simply a matter of doing the best he can for the group as a whole with strictly impartial justice—and so of finding the best possible distribution from this "social point of view." Thus from the arbiter's angle these results have the following appearance:

	The Party Who Fares Best Obtains	The Party Who Fares Second Best Obtains
1.	+170	−10
2.	+150	+20
3.	+100	+50
4.	+100	+40
5.	+ 80	+70

The arbiter would now reason as follows:

(i) No. 3 is preferable to No. 4 by simple dominance. (No one fares worse, some fare better.)

(ii) No. 5 is preferable to No. 3, because it divides the same pool of 150 units more equitably.

(iii) No. 5 is preferable to No. 1, because No. 1 obtains an insubstantially greater *average* benefit (80 versus 75 units) by exacting a massive sacrifice from the person who fares the worst, as compared with how he would fare otherwise; put figuratively, No. 1 enriches the rich at the too drastic expense of the poor.

(iv) The real choice thus lies between No. 2 and No. 5, a comparison in which No. 5 would presumably prevail by reasoning analogous to case (iii).

In general, in a two-person situation the arbiter

(1) By indifference regards a/b as equivalent to b/a in all circumstances

(2) By benevolence prefers both $a+c/b$ and $a/b+c$ to

a/b (with c positive) in all circumstances

(3) By a combination of indifference and benevolence always prefers a more even distribution of the same total amount (and even prefers a significantly more even distribution of a somewhat lesser amount)

These principles, though necessary to an adequate account of the *modus operandi* of the sort of arbitration at issue, are clearly not sufficient. It remains to give an ampler indication of the principles with reference to which the arbitrator sets about his work.

But what manner of decision-rule governs the arbitrator's awards? By what mode of calculation is he to decide which alternative within a group of distributions is to be regarded as preferable? The various principles enumerated thus far do not fix one specific decision-rule, they leave various alternatives. Thus one possible principle of resolution, familiar from the theory of games, lies in the product maximization (thus x/y is preferable to u/v if $x \cdot y > u \cdot v$).[2] A variant approach can be based on the concept of an "effective average," as explored elsewhere by the present writer.[3] But we need not settle this issue here. From our perspective, the divergences among such decision-rules are inessential refinements in sophistication that do not affect essentials. As for the central issues—those on which one's "moral intuitions" are reasonably clear—all such rules are in fundamental agreement. The crucial and overriding consideration is that some device along these lines is needed for taking explicit account of the social point of view in conflict-of-interest situations. The precise form of the rule is a matter of refinement of detail, which can be set aside for present purposes.

To clarify the nature of the arbitrational approach, it is illuminating to contrast it with other modes of "solution" to social-interaction situations involving a conflict of interests. To

2. For the measure at issue here, see J. F. Nash, "The Bargaining Problem," *Econometrica*, 18 (1950): 115–62, and J. C. Harsanyi, "Approach to the Bargaining Problem Before and After the Theory of Games: A Critical Discussion of Zeuthen's, Hicks' and Nash's Theories," *Econometrica*, 24 (1956): 144–57.

3. See N. Rescher, *Distributive Justice* (New York, 1966), which provides a general survey of problems arising in the ethics of distribution. It also provides a clearer view of the general principles which rationalize the decisions of the sort of arbiter we have in mind here.

begin with, it should be said that an impartial arbitrator's settlement may contrast sharply with the results the parties would arrive at if a settlement were made by outright negotiation. By hypothesis, the arbitrator is to proceed solely in terms of the relative merit of the outcome for "the general good," without any concern for the bargaining strength of the participants. To see clearly what this involves, let us introduce an idea of *threat-posture*.

Consider the game

X $\diagdown$ Y	y_1	y_2
x_1	4/1	1/6
x_2	3/0	3/0

Note that in a negotiation X can force Y to select y_1 by X's threatening to go to x_2 (with an assured gain of $+3$), which would result in freezing Y out at 0. Y cannot effectively counterthreaten to go to y_2, since X will simply reply by "playing nasty" at x_2. Thus in a negotiation X can constrain $x_1 y_1$, with a result of 4/1.

On the other hand, note that if there were no communication whatever, and each player had to proceed in complete ignorance of the other's choice, Y would surely opt for y_2, where he is in no case worse off than at y_1, regardless of X's choice. And X would presumably have to "play safe" at x_2. Consequently, $x_2 y_2 (3/0)$ is the virtually certain outcome of prudential choices made without communication. On the other hand, an impartial arbitrator will select $x_1 y_2$, since for him 1/6 is (by strict impartiality) equivalent to 6/1, which is preferable to any other resolution.

We thus arrive at three different solutions:

(1) Strictly impartial arbitration: $x_1 y_2$ (1/6)
(2) Negotiation: $x_1 y_1$ (4/1)
(3) Game-theoretic resolution (without communication): $x_2 y_2$ (3/0)

It is, in this context, worth considering the following game-situation:

X ⟍ Y	y_1	y_2
x_1	2/1	1/3
x_2	1/0	1/0

Here, by reasoning analogous to that of the preceding case, we see that X can compel Y to y_1, so as to produce the result $x_1 y_1$ (2/1). But if there is no communication, Y would opt for y_2 (where he is never worse off than at y_1) and X would opt for x_1 (where he is never worse off than at x_2). The result would be $x_1 y_2$ (1/3). Thus Y stands to lose and X to gain by entering into negotiation. We have here a clear counterexample to invalidate a naive tendency to think that negotiations and the exchange of information must prove mutually advantageous to the parties of a conflict-of-interest situation.

It is a generally recognized truth that voting need not lead to a socially optimal result, but we now see that the same is true of negotiation. As economists have increasingly emphasized, no "hidden hand" assures that individual decisions in conflict-of-interest situations, made from the standpoint of rational self-interest alone, must result in a solution that is optimal from the social point of view. (In this regard, traditional liberal ideology is just as deficient as the economics of the old school.)

Now it is, of course, perfectly possible than an arbitrator should say to himself: "I ought not do less for someone than he could reasonably be expected to do on his own in a negotiation. I must thus take the relative threat-posture of the interested parties into account. in my decision." The arbitrator would therefore conceive his mission in terms of expediting (and perhaps rationalizing) a negotiation among the parties. But this approach is to be excluded by our assumptions. We propose to construe impartiality in a very strict sense, to comprise indifference not only to persons but to the circumstances of threat-potential as well. Our strictly impartial arbiter is to look solely to the desirability of the overall result from "the social point of view," without regard to the relative strength of bargaining positions that may point to an alternative inferior from this social standpoint. He is concerned solely with *realizing the general social advantage,* and in its interest he is prepared to discount claims that reflect advantages in "bargaining strength" that may be built into the structure of the competitive situation.

The sort of arbitration envisaged here is definitely based upon a certain postulated ethical posture on the arbitrator's part: he must be impartial between the parties, benevolent toward them, morally sensitive in appraising the bearing of relevant considerations from their point of view, and capable of taking into proper account both their felt interests and their real interests. Thus he must bring to the problem a moral attitude of a rather demanding sort.

It seems worth pointing out, however, that some of the practical advantages of arbitration are relatively independent of this choice of a particular moral stance, and would, for example, attach also to the dealings of an arbitrator who provides the "moral equivalent" of a negotiation. For here the arbiter is a mere expediter of negotiation, who in his mind enacts a shadow bargaining between the parties. Such arbitration is less costly, less time consuming, and less abrasive and destructive of good will than an actual negotiation. It enjoys also the advantage of removing any need to have threats made in the course of negotion carried out at least partially to establish "credibility." But our present concern is not with such practical advantages of arbitration in general but with the theoretical advantage from "the social point of view" of an arbitration that proceeds on the basis of a particular moral position.

We have established two points:

(1) Arbitration represents a form of communication between the interested parties. Its outcome may well lead to a result different from that at which they would arrive under conditions of complete uncertainty about the actions of the other parties.

(2) There are two distinguishable and potentially divergent modes of "arbitration," one that simply reverts to the type of a rational negotiation, with the arbiter merely serving in the role of a negotiation expediter, and the other where the arbiter is a distinct force, representing the social point of view by aiming at a strictly impartial benevolence (in our somewhat technical sense). Since the former species is simply a negotiation-by-proxy, we shall henceforth reserve the term "arbitration" for the latter alone.[4]

4. This sort of purely moral and apolitical (because power-ignoring) arbitration may not always be the most desirable sort—it may often be impracticable, simply because one of the other parties may refuse to submit to it, since elements of its bargaining strength may be discounted. Nevertheless, it is this sort of

The question however remains: Do the principles laid down here merely *condition* the arbiter's approach or do they actually *determine* it? Could the arbiter simply be replaced by a duly programmed computer? Certainly not. For while his response must in part reflect an automatic response to such considerations, as we have just stressed, they will also in part demand an ethically informed weighing of the conflicting demands of utility assessments, fairness, justice, affective relationships, etc. As we shall see, the arbiter must operate within the framework of a morally informed, overarching vision of the social good, about whose nature we shall have occasion to say more in chapter 6. The arbiter, after all, is not simply a tie-breaker between ultimately indifferent alternatives—on the analogy of a coin toss. His awards must implement a moral rationale that other rational adjudicators would also accept—except, perhaps, for a possible (and always small) area of genuinely indifferent alternatives.

POSSIBLE ADVANTAGES OF ARBITRATION AND THE SOCIAL POINT OF VIEW

Under what sorts of circumstances would a party to a conflict of interest—whose motivation, so we shall assume, is dictated wholly by narrow self-interest—be inclined to agree to arbitration? Clearly, someone would *not* agree to arbitration if he could assure himself by unilateral action of a personally beneficial result that he might well fail to realize in arbitration. Thus consider the following game-situation:

X＼Y	y_1	y_2
x_1	4/1	4/1
x_2	3/4	3/5

Clearly, X will not budge from x_1. An impartial arbitrator might well (nay must) insist on x_2, since for him $3/5$ is equivalent to $5/3$, which is superior to $4/1$. Thus the arbitrator would

---

"strictly ethical" arbitration that we shall need to invoke in the context of our present purposes. To say this is, of course, *not* to deny that the more *realpolitisch* mode of arbitration may prove a most useful means of conflict avoidance.

certainly select $x_2\,y_2$, and X would assuredly lose by arbitration.

Again, given an option, a participant would decline arbitration if he would thereby forgo the prospect of negotiation from a position of strength. A strictly impartial arbitrator might fail to give him the advantage deriving from his threat-posture. (We have already illustrated this case.)

The upshot of these considerations can be summarized by saying that a strictly self-interested party to a conflict-of-interest situation of the type with which we have been concerned would rationally *not* be warranted, and so presumably would not be inclined, to enter into impartial arbitration if either of the following circumstances were to obtain:

(1) He could reasonably expect to do better if there were no communication at all than he would by resorting to arbitration.

(2) He could reasonably expect to do better in a direct negotiation, because he could then act from a position of strength by utilizing his threat-posture.

The sort of arbitration envisaged here is highly committal as to the posture of the arbitrator (impartiality, benevolence, moral sensitivity to both felt and genuine interests, etc.). The principles on which the arbiter is to proceed are all too clear; and anyone— the parties themselves included—can readily check (within limits) on the arbiter's correct use of these principles. For this very reason the parties may well be reluctant to enter into arbitration when "they can see the handwriting on the wall"—to the effect that a result arrived at by other means would be more favorable to themselves than the arbiter's award.

However, there are many cases where arbitration is an attractively self-interest-serving prospect, for a variety of reasons. For example, arbitration might create the possibility for all parties to realize a position certainly no worse and possibly better than that which they would realize if left to themselves. Thus consider

X\ Y	y_1	y_2
x_1	2/10	2/2
x_2	0/0	10/2

Without communication, each would "play safe" and arrive

at $x_1 y_2$ (2/2). Negotiation could well lead to an impasse between $x_1 y_1$ (2/10) and $x_2 y_2$ (10/2). By looking to the arbitrator to make the (now essentially arbitrary) award, each player obtains a hope of gain, and does so without possible cost to himself.

In another interesting family of cases, arbitration is preferable to action without communication because there is a danger that in so proceeding the participants could "outsmart themselves" by being too greedy. Consider

X $\diagdown$ Y	y_1	y_2
x_1	6/4	0/0
x_2	4/4	4/6

X might reason: "Y will certainly play safe at y_1 rather than risk losing an assured payoff of at least 4. So I might as well go for the extra 2 units at x_1." If Y reasons analogously, a mutual catastrophe will result. Arbitration can avoid this unpalatable eventuation.

The prospect of arbitration grows increasingly attractive as the participants run a risk of "castastrophe" by acting in an unconcerted way. (The prisoner's dilemma problem is a clear illustration of this circumstance.) Indeed, it is at such junctures that we find the clearest rationale of social interventionism. If the parties concerned are left "to fight it out for themselves," they will succeed only in damaging their own interests (and conceivably those of innocent bystanders as well). From the angle of the best interests of all concerned, an "imposed" solution may be the most attractive alternative.

Often arbitrative solutions may also have marked advantages over those arrived at through negotiation. For in negotiation a participant must make—and to a degree make good—his threats, and this process may hurt not only innocent bystanders (for example, the general public in a labor dispute) but the parties themselves.

These considerations, then, indicate some of the conditions under which binding arbitration would be the rational resolution from a participant's point of view—namely, to assure himself of an optimal (or perhaps merely a very attractive) result that is not obtainable by independent action. In particular, arbitration looks very attractive when the participants run a substantial risk of serious loss by independent action. Of course, where this circumstance is not inherent in the situation it could, in principle, be brought about artificially through sanctions created by "the society at large."

INTERNALIZATION OF THE WELFARE OF OTHERS AS A SHIFT TOWARD THE ARBITRATOR'S APPROACH

The situation that results in conflict-of-interest cases will, of course, become drastically altered when the individuals concerned are not "economic men" of the traditional sort, actuated by narrow self-interest alone, but rather are in some degree unselfish and *internalize* the benefits to another as part of their own benefit. Assume we confront the following game as representing the *prima facie* conflict situation:

X \ Y	y_1	y_2
x_1	110/60	100/61
x_2	111/50	100/50

If the two parties here make their choices in unwitting independence of each other, the presumptive solution is that X will insist upon x_2 (where he never loses *vis-à-vis* x_1) and Y will insist upon y_2 (where he never loses *vis-à-vis* y_1). By absence of communication they lose the opportunity to realize $x_1 y_1$, where *both* would gain, and arrive at what is the worst possible solution for themselves.

But now suppose that each valued the advantage to another as a small benefit to himself—say at 10 percent thereof. The resulting derivative game will take the form

X \ Y	y_1	y_2
x_1	116/71	106/71
x_2	116/61	105/60

Now the outcome—when there is no communication—is determined through the consideration that both participants would in *this* case prefer their *first* alternative on grounds similar to those considered before, so that $x_1 y_1$ would result. In this case the chances of arriving at a socially more advantageous situation are significantly bettered.

This abstract example puts into vivid relief the significant fact that in conflict-of-interest situations in which the participants are prepared to be at least *somewhat* unselfish—and adopt the social point of view at least to some degree—the prospects of a better realization of the general welfare can often be improved—an improvement that may well also result in a better realization of even the selfish interests of the parties concerned. For an internalization of the welfare of others alters the situation in the direction of the arbitrator's approach. But is this result inevitable? The question arises: By internalizing positively, can we ever arrive at a result that is *socially* inferior from a self-interest-oriented point of view? The answer is again affirmative.

Consider a society of three people in which X alone internalizes (at +50 percent), Y and Z being indifferent. Then consider a case of a choice between two alternatives:

	I	II
X	+15	−10
Y	−10	+10
Z	−10	−10

This transforms into the following tabulation of second-order utilities when the vicarious affects are taken into account:

	I	II
X	+ 5	−10
Y	−10	+10
Z	−10	−10

In the original situation, alternative I is manifestly superior; in the revised situation, alternative II is. Thus we are constrained to recognize that the operation of vicarious affects can also produce a result that represents a socially inferior alternative.

Moreover, we have insisted that there will be some cases where one arrives at an *individually* inferior result by internalizing positively. Thus consider a situation where X must choose between two alternatives:

	Alternative I	Alternative II
X	+8	+10
Y	−5	−30

Suppose X internalizes Y's condition at 10 percent. Then the valuation of the alternatives is transformed into

	I	II
X	+7.5	+ 7
Y	−5	−30

On this revised perspective, X is led to alternative I by dominance considerations (since everyone fares better than under II). Here X "pays a price" for internalization, because *from the standpoint of the first-order situation* he (X) fares less well in I than in II (namely, +8 as contrasted with +10).

These considerations give special point to the question of the linkage subsisting between the vicarious affects and the approach to conflict resolution through impartial arbitration designed to promote the general interest. We noted at the outset that there would be circumstances in which an individual's self-interests would be so at odds with those of others that he would be advisedly reluctant to entrust the issue to an arbiter concerned to promote "the general good" in an impartial way. But to the extent that he internalizes the welfare-condition of others through the operation of the vicarious affects, such a situation becomes less likely, because the sharp edges of the first-level conflict become smoothed at the second level. As individuals come to operate under conditions of greater affective interrelationship, the arbitrative approach to conflict resolution in general becomes more and more acceptable because the "social point of view" it implements becomes an increasingly pronounced facet of the value structure of the individuals themselves.

But, of course, the path of arbitrative resolution can be smoothed by an outright consilience of narrow self-interest as well as by the development of affective community. This important prospect must be given the detailed consideration it deserves.

PRESSURES TOWARD THE SOCIAL POINT OF VIEW

We have seen that choice based on a positive internalization of the welfare of others *may, but need not,* be productive of self-oriented advantage. The benefit to be derived from such internalization thus becomes an issue not of theoretical generality, but of the empirical detail of specific cases. It is certainly possible that the structure of the social-interaction situations in which we find ourselves is such that, *by and large,* a socially minded positive internalization proves generally beneficial from the standpoint of pure self-interest as well. And even though this is true not inevitably but only generally and by and large, it may well be that if one cannot foresee the detailed interaction situations in which he may find himself, then a general policy of the sort of unselfishness at issue in the positive internalization of the welfare-condition of one's fellows may also turn out to be prudent as well.[5]

The aim of the ensuing remarks is to argue that this prospect of the prudential advantageousness of unselfish conduct is actually realized in the empirical circumstances of the present-day condition of our lives.

The mutuality of interests in the massified and systematized society created by advanced technology and increasing populations assures that the public welfare is not only more critical as a social desideratum, but is also rendered easier of attainment by modern social and technical instrumentalities.[6] And this conjoint prospect of realizing increased benefits at relatively decreased cost tends to create pressures for raising the general welfare to a higher place in the spectrum of the social values espoused by individuals. In the final analysis, the social point of view will prevail *because it has to*; that is, because disaster will ensue if it does not. In a complexly articulated mass society, "little" transgressions become amplified through the system (for example, loud talking during a concert, a shout of "fire!" in a crowded theater, massive repetition of "trivial" pollution of the air or water, etc.).

5. See, for example, Bibb Lantane and J. M. Darley, "Bystander 'Apathy,' " *Scientific American* 57 (1969): 244–68.

6. This view and the grounds for it are developed in greater detail in the author's contributions to K. Baier and N. Rescher, eds., *Values and the Future* (New York, 1969).

The mechanism of this presumptive increase in emphasis upon social welfare as a personal value deserves consideration. Adoption of the social point of view is called for by an optimization of self-interest in the context operative under current conditions, and requires for its efficient realization a degree of *internalization* of the welfare of others. This internalization of the general welfare of the group as a personal value continues and extends a wider process of social empathy whose general structure is quite familiar. We marvel nowadays that ordinary, well-meaning people in the eighteenth century could have been so thick-skinned as to attend public executions in the spirit of a circus performance, and without recoiling from what to us would be a virtually unbearable spectacle of human anguish and suffering. Again, we wonder how well-meaning people in the nineteenth century could countenance the noxious effects of personality-destructive mass poverty and grinding privation—accepting this unshrinkingly, sometimes as the inevitable result of Divine Providence, sometimes as the inexorable consequence of economic law. Our society has by gradual, step-by-step internalization transformed into a threat to *self*-interest most kinds of threats to the physical and economic well-being of *other* individuals and groups. In general, the concern for the public welfare, as it has developed in the twentieth century, is only the most comprehensive manifestation of this internalizing process.

Yet this point, although correct, is in a way misleading. It appears to put increased concern for social welfare into the perspective of an increasing enlightenment, a growing acquisition of those virtues (unselfishness, concern for others, nonparochialism) that are the marks of truly civilized men. But to see the matter from this standpoint alone would be to omit the equally important aspect of *narrow* self-interest and selfish need. The conditions operative in modern advanced societies confront us with a system of interlinkages in which, because of functional interdependencies in many spheres of life, the individual cannot achieve his personal welfare-interests without a correlative realization of those of his fellows. Technological advance and economic sophistication, social complexity and urban crowding— these are the operative factors in establishing the prudential urgency of other-regarding considerations. Because of the systematic interrelationships in the medical, economic, social, and educational areas, a man's personal welfare is to be secured in an effective and stable way only through the realization of arrangements that also support the general welfare.

A modern society is an intricate and complex self-maintaining system, or rather a constellation of such systems: political, economic, medical, educational, etc.—as well as systems of transportation, communication, environmental maintenance, and the like. Increasingly, the operating conditions of our contemporary socioeconomic environment create circumstances of interaction and interdependency in which it is only by acting with a view to the interests and advantages of others that our own individual interests and advantages can be achieved. The way in which we act as individuals affects the makeup of our common physical and social environment, the systematic context in which we must all operate, in such a way that if we cause its degradation for some, the network of interconnections is strong enough to assure its degradation for ourselves as well.

The tendency of these considerations is clear: the general welfare, and consequently the "welfare of others," is something that can be internalized and made part of "one's own welfare" in an enlarged sense. Moreover, circumstances can be realized— and indeed there are pressures at work to make them actual in an increasingly emphatic way—in which this seemingly disinterested basis of action will in fact produce results that are selfishly advantageous as well.

The upshot of this discussion is that while the personal advantageousness of the social point of view is by no means an inherently *necessary* phenomenon, the important fact remains that the contingent circumstances of the present era are such that it can reasonably be supposed to prove generally advantageous. And at the level of society as a whole, the lesson is clear: it has come to be a prime desideratum to shape a system of sanctions, incentives, and penalties of such a sort that, for people in general, action from narrow self-interest and action from public interest may be assimilated. Such social engineering as the political process admits should, under these conditions, be so deployed as to shape the communal operating environment so that actions against the public interest also militate against the agent's private interest.

To be sure, a person can exhibit a socially benign concern for the welfare of others for markedly distinct reasons: (1) *prudentially* or selfishly, because promotion of the welfare of others represents, for him, a facilitating means to the ulterior goal of his own welfare, or (2) *benevolently* or unselfishly, because the welfare of others is of intrinsic value for him, prized in its own right (without "ulterior motives"). As Kant's insistence on the centrality of the good will rightly stressed, the issue of motivation is crucial to morality and provides a sharp border at the theoretical level to separate morality from mere prudence. But—on the line of reasoning set forth here—this *theoretical* division becomes greatly attenuated at the *practical* level, since under suitable conditions the prudent and the moral thing to do will tend to coincide in actual effect.

Arguments can readily be adduced—and indeed some have been produced in the preceding pages—to show that there is no sound reason or theoretical principle for holding that the dictates of self-oriented prudence and other-concerned morality *must* yield concordant rather than divergent results. But the tendency of these present considerations has been to maintain that, while this remains true at the theoretical level, the actual, empirically given (rather than theoretically inevitable) circumstances of the case represented by the conditions prevailing here and now are in fact such that a convergence is forthcoming. And, given the generally admitted capacity of moral motives to deepen, fortify, and secure the operation of considerations of prudential self-interest, there is good reason why, even from the angle of a rationality narrowly construed in terms of prudential self-interest, a strengthening of the genuinely moral concerns of men for each other should be seen as an eminently rational step.

5

◈ Vicarious Affects and the Critique of Utilitarianism

PRELIMINARY OBSERVATIONS

The workings of the vicarious affects create serious difficulties for a utilitarian approach to moral issues along the lines of the historical tradition from Bentham, via the Mills, to Sidgwick and Smart.[1] It might seem at first glance that a recognition of the vicarious affects would be readily compatible with an orthodox utilitarianism. Indeed, it might be thought that the utilitarian could readily appropriate the entire machinery of affective internalization with the remark: "My theory encounters no difficulties from a recognition of the vicarious affects; it calls on us to base our ethical judgment on a reckoning of utilities, but there is no reason why they could not be of your second-order (post-internalization) sort, rather than the utilities of the more commonly envisaged first-order sort." The aim of this chapter is to drive home the point that, while a "utilitarianism" of this internalization-recognizing sort is not theoretically infeasible, it would have to depart so radically from the tenets of the traditional utilitarian doctrine that it no longer deserves the same name.

"EACH IS TO COUNT FOR ONE, NO ONE FOR MORE THAN ONE"

The central thesis of utilitarian ethics is that the moral rightness of an act is determined by the balance of its good versus bad

1. For a bibliography of utilitarianism see N. Rescher, *Distributive Justice* (New York, 1966).

consequences for the members of the group to which the agent belongs, and that in this calculation the interests of all these members are to count equally. Complete parity must be maintained with respect to all concerned; they must count as altogether equal and must be treated as interchangeable units throughout the operation of the moral calculus. This stance is encapsulated in Jeremy Bentham's well-known dictum "Each is to count for one, no one for more than one." For the utilitarian moralist, the moral worth of an action is determined wholly in terms of its *consequences for the social group,* and in evaluating these consequences the interests of all members of the society are to stand on *an altogether equal footing.*

An acknowledgment of the moral propriety of a differentially operative role for the vicarious affects creates a decisive obstacle to this position. For to recognize the differential operation of the (positive) vicarious affects as ethically legitimate is to take the stance that an agent is not morally obligated to treat all others alike in ethical deliberation, since it is appropriate for him to take the interests of some into account more extensively than those of others. It is not only *excusable* but *morally right* that (for example) a parent should take the interests of his child more seriously and extensively into account than those of a perfect stranger. In its "each counts for one" principle, utilitarian ethics fails to recognize the ethical legitimacy of interpersonal relationships of the type codified in a recognition of the vicarious affects. It acts as though all reference to person-to-person kinships could, nay should, be dismissed as irrelevant from the moral point of view. But this represents the very reverse of the truth.

Conceivably, the greater happiness of a greater number could be served if people lavished upon unknown others the cares, energies, and resources a man devotes to his wife, children, parents, etc., treating as indifferent all special responsibilities assumed or inherited *vis-à-vis* certain persons with whom he stands in relationships of special kinship. But whatever reasons can be urged on behalf of such indifference to natural or social relationships, the defense of *moral* justification is certainly not one of them. Not utilitarian but *ethical* considerations compel the recognition of the vicarious affects.

The crucial point of the differential operation of the vicarious affects is that we cannot with moral propriety ask that a person value the interests (welfare, happiness) of all his fellows equally, as the utilitarian's moral paragon would have him do. To ask this is not theoretically impossible, but morally perverse in its refusal to heed ethically valid relationships among people. (To be sure, it is also unrealistic and impracticable, since it seems to run counter to the actualities of human nature.)

To say all this is not, of course, to say that the even-handedness the utilitarian demands is altogether out of place in human affairs. It is neither practicable nor desirable for the *private* agent acting on his own account and *in propria persona*. But with a *public* agent acting *ex officio* as trustee of the general good, the matter is altogether different. The holder of a public office, such as a legislator, a judge, a government administrator or the like, can, of course, be expected to treat all people alike and to refrain in his official capacity from setting the interests of some above those of others.

The dictum "Treat everyone alike" has long been recognized as a fundamental principle of justice, binding upon those who are its dispensers—which, of course, includes all of us in certain roles and capacities. But this principle of action at the public level certainly will not be of unrestricted applicability in the private transactions of men in the pursuit of their personal and private relations among one another. Thus the stated principle of justice cannot be routinely transposed into a universal principle of morality governing human interactions in general. Justice, after all, aims at no more than establishing certain minima of obligation—morality also recognizes the claims of special relationships in which these minima are greatly transcended.

A crucial flaw of utilitarian ethics—one that a consideration of the vicarious affects clearly brings to light—inheres in the fact that one must not generalize the ethical propriety of the indifferently even-handed approach of the official acts of public agents to gainsay the propriety of a suitably articulated person-differentiating approach in the personal interactions of private individuals. The utilitarian's indifferentialist approach makes the mistake of transposing the standards of justice in a public agency into standards of individual ethics and personal morality.

Moreover, even here, at the level of choices of someone who acts on behalf of the public in general (such as a legislator), it is presumably only *his own* vicarious affects that are to be discounted, not those of people in general. That is, the legislator should, *ex officio*, suppress recognition of his own special relationships to people—though not necessarily theirs to one another. Thus consider a microsociety of three persons, X, Y, Z, two of whom, X and Y, are sympathetically oriented toward each other (say at a positive p.t.r. of 50 percent). Suppose that two policies lie open that will produce the indicated *prima facie* (first-order) results regarding utility gains/losses:

	Alternative I	Alternative II
X	+ 0	+ 0
Y	+10	+ 4
Z	+ 2	+10

Once the vicarious affects are taken account of (at the indicated rate), the utility situation regarding these two alternatives is transformed into

	I	II
X	+ 5	+ 2
Y	+10	+ 4
Z	+ 2	+10

Let us now view these alternatives from a socially impersonal point of view, as follows:

	I	II
The best off	+10	+10
The next best off	+ 5	+ 4
The worst off	+ 2	+ 2

The upshot is clear: policy I definitely prevails on the basis of straightforward dominance considerations.

To be sure, if we appoint X as *ex officio* arbiter of the general good, then—since he is, by hypothesis, to act disinterestedly—we must recalculate on the basis that his vicarious affects are to be discounted, and that he is not to be allowed to let his special relationship to Y enter the calculation. We again obtain

	I	II
X	+ 0	+ 0
Y	+10	+ 4
Z	+ 2	+10

And the situation, from a socially impersonal point of view, now decisively favors II on the basis of dominance considerations.

To recognize the role of the vicarious affects is therefore not to rule out a purely impersonal assessment of alternatives from the social point of view; rather, it is to insist upon postponing this assessment until after the differentiating effects of the vicarious affects have been taken into appropriate account. When acting in a public rather than a private capacity—as a public trustee rather than as a private individual—an agent should discount the operation of the vicarious affects in special cases (preeminently his own). And the preceding example shows clearly that it will not do to take the view that—even after we allow the entry of the vicarious affects—the legislator should continue to take *everyone* into account equally, himself included. For in his official capacity he is constrained to ignore the operation of the vicarious affects when they would lead him to favor those who stand in some special relationship to himself. (But, of course, this fact that certain persons [public agents] are duty bound—in acting *ex officio*—to ignore the operation of the vicarious affects in certain cases does not tend to show that the vicarious affects as such are ethically illegitimate and ineligible for entry into moral calculation.)

At this stage, let us dispose of one possible line of objection. Someone might argue as follows:

> The thesis that a given person is warranted in differentially treating other persons in some category, *C*, does not really go against the dictum to treat everyone alike. For this now survives in the form:
>
> > For any person *x*: if *x* belongs to category *C*, he is to be treated in manner *M*.
>
> And the principle of treating all alike clearly survives in this universally conditional form of the precept at issue.

Someone might therefore argue that the "differentiating" force of the vicarious affects is only spuriously differential. But this will not do. The key question is whether *hypothetical* or *categorical* uniformity is at issue. For someone can always introduce a spurious parity of treatment by shifting to an if-then rationale of procedure.

Thus contrast the following two theses:

(1) *Since X is* my child (parent, patient, employee, etc.), I am obliged to do such-and-such things for him (which I would not be obliged to do for *Y* or *Z*, who does not fall into this category).

(2) *If X were* my child (parent, patient, employee, etc.), I would be obliged to do such-and-such things for him (which I would not necessarily be called on to do for someone who does not fall into this category).

The former thesis stipulates a differential mode of treatment of people in a certain group *G*, in an assertoric and categorical way; the second proceeds conditionally and hypothetically. Now in this conditional and hypothetical way we can always introduce the spurious generality of saying of *anyone* at all that IF he were a member of group *G*, THEN he would—universally, regardless of who he might be—qualify as beneficiary of my obligation. But it is clear that this hypothetical generality—a generality that casts membership in *G* in the role of a universally operative condition—is simply a spurious way of introducing universality into a situation that is fundamentally nonuniversal, differential, and selectively preferential. In such cases, hypothetical conditionalization achieves a merely spurious generality by verbal "sleight of hand."

Quite patently, the precept

"Honor thy father and thy mother"

which on its very surface places certain persons in a special category deserving differential treatment, can be recast into the logically equivalent form

$(\forall x)([(x$ is your father) v $(x$ is your mother)$] \rightarrow x$ is to be honored by you).

I grant the equivalence willingly, but insist that its substance is altogether incapable of bearing the burden it is asked to carry. The very triviality of the logical legerdemain that underlies this equivalence indicates that the seemingly universalized version is only a *fradulent* universalization that lies at the logical surface and does not cut through to the core of the issue.

In short, if *this* way of departicularizing a differential precept is to count as constituting a genuine generalization, this whole issue of generalization has been reduced to a pointless quibble.

(The vacuity of the fradulent universalization of the principle "Treat everyone alike" seems to me in effect equivalent with Hegel's contention [*Encyclopaedia*, § 539] that "equality before the law" is a purely formal and largely empty precept, because in practice the circumstances in which laws apply "presuppose unequal conditions" and, accordingly, envisage "unequal legal circumstances and duties"—for example, between the several parties to a contract.)

To recognize the authority of the vicarious affects is to admit the propriety of a differential treatment of people in the framework of moral calculation, and to concede the legitimacy of treating certain people (parents, children, friends, colleagues) in a way different from others. To be sure, one can insist on finding a makeshift universality here if one wants to be doctrinaire about it. Instead of conceding a special obligation to a particular individual (for example, one's parent), one could insist on a general obligation toward *anyone* at all—provided he meet the special condition of being one's parent. But the very fact that the *application* of such a general rule to those who do not meet its condition requires such "far-out" (implausible, actuality-remote) hypotheses (for example, that yonder small child be my parent) marks the generalization as spurious.

Of course, the utilitarian might yet object as follows to our insistence on the moral justifiability of person-differentiating principles of action:

You claim that a fraudulent universalization is involved in treating (say) "Honor thy father and thy mother" as a precept telling us how to treat people in general. But if everyone has counted for one and nobody for more than one in the *justification* of such a precept, why should a utilitarian care if the rule itself is general or not? As long as its justificatory rationale shows that its observance works for the general good (each counting equally), why worry about its surface-differential aspects?

This objection merely shifts the ground of disagreement back into the terrain of the hypothetical. What if—reality to the contrary notwithstanding—a person-differentiating approach did *not* work for the general good (though not, of course, producing outright disasters)? The utilitarian would reject it—and show thereby that his earlier acceptance was crucially based on merely contingent arrangements. Thus even if the utilitarian is in a position to recognize the vicarious affects as legitimate, this recognition cannot bear the weight of a *moral* legitimation because it hinges on a merely empirical assumption as to how things work in the world. His legitimation is unable to endow person-differentiating considerations with the sort of standing that *as a matter of principle* is ultimately at issue when they are deemed valid on *moral* grounds.

These considerations point to yet another kindred prospect of a strictly utilitarian justification of differential treatment. I have in mind the approach formulated by the judicious Sidgwick,[2] as follows:

Passing to consider how our benevolence ought to be distributed among our fellow-men, we may conveniently make clear the Intuitional view by contrasting it with that of Utilitarianism. For Utilitarianism is sometimes said to resolve all virtue into universal and impartial Benevolence: it does not, however, prescribe that we should love all men equally, but that we should aim at Happiness generally as our ultimate end, and so consider the happiness of any one individual as equally important with the equal happiness of any other, as an element of this total; and should distribute our kindness so as to make this total as great as possible, in whatever way this result may be attained. Practically of course the distribution of any individual's services will, even on this view, be unequal: as each man will obviously promote the general happiness best by rendering services to a limited number, and to some more than others: but the inequality, on the Utilitarian theory, is secondary and derivative. [pp. 241–42]

And Sidgwick then moves on to the obvious point that while, for a utilitarian, the happiness/welfare of every person must *at the theoretical level* be looked on impartially as wholly alike, it must be recognized that, *from a practical standpoint,* a person will be so circumstanced as to be able to contribute far more effectively to the welfare of some than of others. On this basis, the rationale for differential treatment can be sought in the factors of efficiency and effectiveness. We are simply in a better position to contribute to the welfare of those who are "close" to us. A utilitarian can surely *divide* the task of increasing welfare by recognizing various stations and their person-differentiating duties.[3]

2. Henry Sidgwick, *The Methods of Ethics*, 7th ed. (London, 1907).
3. *Ibid.*, p. 252.

However, from the aspect of the moral rationale of the differential treatment inherent in the justification of the vicarious affects, this attenuated utilitarian impartiality, conditioned by rule-utilitarian considerations of efficiency and effectiveness, has numerous shortcomings, among which the following are prominent: (1) It would give top priority to the highly problematic "duties to oneself," since one's effectiveness is presumably maximal at this level. (2) It would make for a systematic difference in our obligations toward those who just happen to be more accessible (all else being equal). (3) When all else is *not* equal, it makes for counterintuitive priorities of obligation (for example, a man may well be in a position to promote the welfare of his employees more effectively than that of his children, but this would not ordinarily be taken to mean that the former override the latter).

But the crucial point is this: even if one could justify on utilitarian principles the *practice* of treating people differentially (supposedly because this is maximally efficient in conducing to the good of all), this defense leaves us with an essentially contingent justification: "As things tend to work in the world, this *modus operandi* leads to the goal of . . ." No moralist who regards differential obligations as a feature noncontingently inherent in the ethical ramifications of human relationships could accept this approach. As with any circumstantially grounded rule of thumb, the issue of its applicability *in the present case* will always crop up. And even if it does not arise explicitly, it is always tacitly present in the background, posing issues that, however conveniently ignored for practical purposes, can never be laid to rest at the level of theoretical principle and accordingly cannot provide the sort of properly *moral* justification that is demanded.

The attempt to distinguish between respectable (rule-reinforced) and unrespectable (rule-unrecognized) utilities on the basis that the former are somehow fertile and the latter sterile thus comes to shipwreck. It does so because the whole issue of efficacy in fostering the further realization of utility crucially pivots the discussion on the question of the working conditions and circumstances under which the promotion of certain utility-considerations *are causally operative* in their utility-fostering or-retarding results. And on this basis fertility can never be transmuted into the sort of validating principle required to warrant moral distinctions.

"But surely," it might be argued, "the utilitarian can admit the need *to teach a moral code,* both to support desirable (welfare-promotive) motivations to action and to simplify moral calculation. And, accordingly, the utilitarian can recognize stable rules that carry special and differential duties and responsibilities toward duly correlative persons." So far so good. But what is to be the *nature* of this moral code, which on the one hand meets utilitarian desiderata and on the other underwrites the vicarious affects? Our thesis is that if it is to do an adequate job at the latter, it cannot be a utilitarian morality. This would be fatal. For it would surely put the utilitarian in an untenable position to concede that his moral theory is not self-sustaining, that it enjoins him to teach and foster a moral theory at variance with itself.

"THE GREATEST HAPPINESS OF THE GREATEST NUMBER"

Two Types of Utilitarianism

By the very nature of the program he espouses, the utilitarian is committed to the maximization of utility (welfare, happiness, or whatever). But how are we to construe the utility that is at issue here? Is only immediate self-interested and selfish "utility" at issue or also the wider and fuller range of the vicarious affects? We thus reach the fundamental question: Is the utilitarian to admit or exclude the operation of the vicarious affects in the assessment of individual utility?

Depending upon how we resolve this fundamental question, two forms of utilitarianism confront us: that which admits and that which excludes the vicarious affects—let us dub them A-utilitarianism (*A* for "admitting") and O-utilitarianism (*O* for "omitting"), respectively. Either way, the issue is not the procedural *structure* of the utilitarian calculations but the *very meaning of the utility-values* that are to figure in them. Are the utilities to be constituted in the other-regarding fashion that is necessary if the vicarious affects are to be taken into account, or are they not?

Each of these two versions of utilitarian theory suffers from significant defects. Let us first consider O-utilitarianism.

To begin with, it must be emphasized that the utilitarian would assume an untenable position in discounting the vicarious affects by dismissing them as beside the point for his problems. One cannot avoid recognizing as an established fact of human nature that people actually do participate in the welfare of others by way of sympathy and antipathy, kinship and estrangement. And the reality of this phenomenon certainly affects the evaluation of utilities. Thus in a microsociety of four individuals, A, B, C, and D, two of whom (A and B) are disposed toward each other in an affectively positive way (say at a p.t.r. of 20 percent), the two *prima facie* utility distributions

	Alternative I	Alternative II
A	+20	0
B	+20	0
C	0	+21
D	0	+21

are such that alternative II seems at first sight (socially) superior to I (and is undoubtedly so if the vicarious affects are discounted).

But when they are taken into account, we arrive at the transformed situation

	Alternative I	Alternative II
A	$+20 + \frac{1}{5}(+20) = +24$	0
B	$+20 + \frac{1}{5}(+20) = +24$	0
C	0	+21
D	0	+21

Once the vicarious affects are taken into account, the preferability situation is reversed. Thus there is no gainsaying the difference the vicarious affects can make within the framework of utilitarian calculation.

But while the vicarious affects cannot be dismissed on *factual* grounds of making no real difference to the *de facto* arrangements of utility distribution, it might be contended that they should be dismissed on *normative* grounds, as being illegitimate or improper, and thus be discounted in ethical analysis. Though this position is, as noted above, justified with respect to the specifically *antipathetical* vicarious affects, it is certainly not warranted with respect to the vicarious affects in general. Quite the contrary. The man who does not participate positively in the utility (welfare, happiness) of certain of his fellows—whose own stock of utility is not diminished by the ill fate of his proximate fellows (his kindred, friends, associates) and augmented by their good fortune—is not a moral exemplar but an inhuman monster. And much the same goes for the man whose welfare is in substantial measure augmented by the illfare of others. We not only can but must take the vicarious affects into appropriate account in ethical analysis.

This line of though applies with special force to utilitarianism. For the utilitarian, utility is a gift horse he cannot look in the mouth. The utilitarian has to take his utilities as he finds them—the very structure of his theory precludes him from dismissing *any* utilities as undeserving of a place in the calculation. Thus, given the fact that the utilities of people can depend on those of others, the utilitarian has no alternative but to accept the resulting utility readjustments at face value. The normative dismissal or discounting of admittedly genuine utilities is not an option open to utilitarianism.

The utilitarian cannot distinguish between good and bad utilities, selecting some as meriting encouragement and rejecting others as deserving deemphasis. (To be sure, Bentham stressed the *fertility* of modes of pleasure as a means for facilitating other pleasures. And perhaps on this basis someone might argue that malicious pleasures will get a low ranking in the utility calculus as compared with others. But this is surely a two-edged sword. Given the extent to which malice breeds on malice and envy on envy, it would be most problematic to hold that, where the transfer of utility by the vicarious affects is concerned, the boundaries of the fertile/sterile division run parallel with the positive/negative.) To be sure, a utilitarian can work to create a society where *Schadenfreude* is not the best or highest sort of pleasure, but there remains the fundamental problem of showing *why he should want to do so on strictly utilitarian principles.*

So much, then, for the critique of an O-utilitarianism that seeks to dismiss the vicarious affects from its assessment of personal utilities. Let us now consider an A-utilitarianism that is prepared to admit them.

The most striking demerit of an A-utilitarian admission of the vicarious affects at their face value inheres in its recognition of the negative affects. It gives envy, jealousy, and ill-will a weight they do not deserve in ethical analysis. Let us return to the example considered in chapter 2—a micro-society of five individuals of mutually antipathetic inclination (say at a negative p.t.r. of 30 percent)—and compare two redistributions of utility:

	I	II
A	+10	−10
B	+10	−10
C	+10	−10
D	+10	−10
E	+10	−10

After allowing for the effect of the specified vicarious affects, we obtain

	I	II
A	−2	+2
B	−2	+2
C	−2	+2
D	−2	+2
E	−2	+2

It is clearly absurd that an analysis of the ethical proprieties of the case should recognize as a comparative social advantage a change purchased at the cost of what is (objectively speaking) a detriment to the welfare of all involved.

We arrive at a dilemma: (1) An A-utilitarian acceptance of the vicarious affects commits the misstep of recognizing the negative ones, which do not deserve such recognition. (2) An O-utilitarian dismissal of the vicarious affects commits the misstep of rejecting the positive ones, which do merit recognition. The utilitarian approach is in trouble either way. The vicarious affects are of particular relevance for utilitarianism because they indicate the crucial importance of drawing and maintaining a line with which utilitarianism cannot come to terms on its own ground.

The crucial point is not that the utilitarian is unable to establish a taxonomy of different sorts of utilities but, rather, that he is unable to deploy his utilitarian apparatus to underwrite distinctions that must, as a matter of principle, be brought to bear on the ethical evaluation of utilities themselves. The question whether or not utilities are to be so construed as to take account of the vicarious affects poses issues that press beyond the boundaries of the utilitarian program and cannot be resolved within its limits.

Prospects of a Utilitarian Reduction

The differential treatment by an individual of the welfare-interests of others might conceivably be defended as a viable policy *within* the framework of orthodox utilitarian considerations. The utilitarian would thus be able to achieve the needed *via media*, intermediate between the automatic acceptance and the automatic omission of the vicarious affects. This tactic is a utilitarian *reductionism* that insists that the "right" (that is, positive) vicarious affects can be justified *derivatively* in orthodox utilitarian terms, and thus need not be recognized as specifically distinct factors. This approach would presumably rely on the argument that it works out best for the (impersonally considered) general welfare of the members of a society if each member acts on such a parochial basis.

Now even on the surface, this line of argument is not very promising. For how could the social optimization of individual parochialism be guaranteed? Such a utilitarian version of the hidden-hand theory of nineteenth-century *laisser-faire* economics is every bit as problematic and implausible as its original analogue.

Let us examine more closely the sort of argument at issue. It proceeds along the following lines:

> Utilitarian theory need make no special provision for the vicarious affects, because they are readily accommodated in the general framework of the traditional, orthodox theory. That a man should participate in the welfare of his fellows is a circumstance that redounds to the general good, and is, accordingly, rather a consequence of utilitarianism than an obstacle to it.

But this contention that an internalization-recognizing utilitarianism can be reduced to an internalization-ignoring one at the level of universalized policy cannot be given an adequate theoretical justification. For consider a highly "deprived" microsociety of individuals whose utility circumstances are uniformly negative. In such a case, if each individual participates positively (sympathetically) in the fate of his fellows at a positive p.t.r., we obtain the second-order result that everyone fares very badly indeed—far worse than if there were no mutual sympathy, or indeed antagonism. As this example shows, under such utility-impoverished conditions *everyone* fares worse under circumstances of participatory communion. (Among mutually sympathetic persons, one will clearly obtain the *reverse* of the "misery loves company" phenomenon.)

Thus, instead of countenancing and commending affective participation on a utilitarian basis, one arrives—in all such situations of utility-deprivation—at the consequence that a utilitarian analysis would condemn the (positive) vicarious affects out of hand, as working to the detriment of "the greatest happiness of the greatest number." For clearly in all those cases (perhaps rather common than otherwise) where the bulk of our fellows fare ill, it works to the *disadvantage* of the general good that this fact should be taken—through sympathy—as a basis for diminishing one's own sense of well-being. It is a mistake to hold that the needed accommodation of the vicarious affects can be legitimated on utilitarian lines because "it redounds to the general good that a man should participate in the welfare of his fellows."

The "no man is an island" line of thought, that the happiness of a person requires involvement with the happiness of others, does not afford an adequate utilitarian defense of the positive affects. For while these affects certainly increase a man's *potential* for achieving happiness, they equally augment his potential for *un*happiness. They operate even-handedly on both sides of the issue of utility-augmentation.

It might, however, be argued that this overlooks the factor of *incentive*: that if we pay a price for the utility-deprivation of others we would be motivated to work for their relief, and so produce a significant improvement in the utility-condition of people-in-general. This dynamic, motivational aspect of the vicarious affects must certainly be admitted and accorded the importance it deserves. But, taken as a generalized argument that the greatest-happiness principle underwrites the positive affects, it shatters on the tragic aspect of the human condition that, under many sorts of circumstances, vicarious sympathy is totally *impotent* from the standpoint of happiness-improvement because, under the circumstances, nothing can be done to mend matters.

Moreover, the crucial difference in legitimacy between the positive and the negative vicarious affects cannot be suitably rationalized on a utilitarian basis. The positive affects certainly cannot be legitimated on the utilitarian grounds that their operation is inevitably happiness-conducive. Consider the basic situation of a microsociety of three utility-deprived members, faced with the following distribution of utilities, subject to an assumed p.t.r. of +20 percent:

$$X \quad -10$$
$$Y \quad -10$$
$$Z \quad -10$$

After introducing the workings of the vicarious affects, one arrives at

$$X \quad -14$$
$$Y \quad -14$$
$$Z \quad -14$$

Since everyone is worse off when the sympathetic affects are admitted into the calculation in such cases, these certainly do not qualify as utility-augmenting in such cases.

Again, the antipathetic affects cannot be invalidated on the utilitarian grounds that their dismissal is utility-decreasing. For consider the following basic situation, subject to an assumed p.t.r. of −20 percent:

$$X \quad -10$$
$$Y \quad -10$$
$$Z \quad -10$$

After introducing the effect of the vicarious affects, we then arrive at

$$X \quad -6$$
$$Y \quad -6$$
$$Z \quad -6$$

Everyone is better off when the antipathetic affects are admitted into the calculation; so they do not warrant dismissal utility-diminishing.

The key fact remains that *moral* considerations require us to discount the antipathetic affects: we cannot rule them out on the utilitarian considerations of functioning so as to make people less happy. In a society in which people in general are envious, a step to the detriment of most may well improve the *felt* condition of all. But such a step is certainly not to be approved on moral grounds. We surely would not, on *moral* grounds, want to promote the hedonic condition of people in this way, degrading their *actual* utility-condition to cater to the malice of their envious fellows. (The alleviation of misery by malice, however understandable, and even excusable, can never be praised or encouraged on moral grounds.)

Still, a supporter of utilitarianism might be tempted to offer the following defense:

> But surely one can use a rule-utilitarian approach to justify the differential treatment at issue in a (properly designed) acknowledgment of the vicarious affects. For presumably the systematic recognition of the admissibility of the sympathetic and a systematic dismissal of the negative vicarious affects would represent a policy conducive to the general advantage of the community.

This line of defense will not serve. It enters the field of contention with too little and too late. The rule-utilitarian calculation at issue must, of course, proceed with reference to the distribution of utilities reached (or presumptively created) by adopting one or the other line of procedure (that is, recognizing or dismissing the vicarious affects in a utility-calculation). A rule-utilitarian approach, accordingly, *cannot avoid begging* the very question at issue in requiring us to proceed by assessing distributions of utility.

Rule-utilitarianism might conceivably be appropriately used to validate the differential treatment of people in *certain* regards, but it cannot be used to validate their differential treatment in a determination of utility-assessments. For these utility-assessments are something we need as appropriate *inputs* in a rule-utilitarian calculation, and, accordingly, such calculations are impotent to render a certification of their appropriateness. Being *presupposed* by the rule-utilitarian calculation, this appropriateness of utility-determinations cannot be made to hinge upon the outcome of such a calculation, it must be resolved *prior* to the calculation. It is obviously inappropriate to maintain that the question of *how* utilitarian calculations are to be made should rest upon utilitarian considerations. The utilitarian theory is thus impotent to help us resolve those specific moral issues posed by the very *modus operandi* of utilitarianism itself.

To say all this is not, of course, to deny that one can adopt a version of utilitarianism that handles the vicarious affects in the "right" and judiciously discriminating way, admitting the positive affects into its assessments of utility and dismissing the negative ones. But the utilitarian who proceeds in this manner must squarely face the fact that this procedure steps outside the rationale of utilitarian theory and involves an appeal to justificatory considerations that go against the grain of orthodox utilitarianism.

Accordingly, the rational evaluation of human actions does not admit an ethical reductivism on the utilitarian model, one that proposes to extract moral considerations from such *prima facie* disjointed factors as happiness or satisfaction or welfare or "utility." Rather—quite in reverse!—the proper assessment of the role of these utilitarian factors demands the introduction of moral considerations for examination, through the familiar dialectic of means and ends that asks whether the realization of these perfectly genuine human values is achieved in the cases at hand by means that are themselves capable of rational justification. One cannot reduce morality to seemingly amoral prudence by extracting it from exclusively utilitarian considerations, because in this context the proper handling of these utilitarian considerations calls for the introduction of moral considerations.

But once the utilitarian model is rejected, the question remains: How is the social good to be calculated? In addressing ourselves to the interests of society we must face this question of how the social good is to be assessed. This larger issue requires a separate treatise; it cannot be dealt with in the narrow limits of the present discussion, and the reader must content himself with a reference to its treatment in another place.[4] It will suffice for our present purposes to observe that much of what is necessary on this head was implicit in the "impartial arbiter's approach"

---

4. See N. Rescher, *Welfare: The Social Issues in Philosophical Perspective* (Pittsburgh, 1972).

of chapter 4. Within the framework of the present discussion, it may be postulated that "the social good" is—generally speaking—to be determined in terms of those principles and guidelines which were stipulated above for the *modus operandi* of an impartial arbiter.[5]

Is Utility Maximization the Right Standard?

These deliberations bring to the fore, with special force and vividness, a very fundamental (though by no means novel) point in the critique of utilitarianism, a point that utilitarian theorists have on occasion recognized but have never really dealt with satisfactorily. Utilitarian theory insists that the ethical merit of an act lies in its effects upon the welfare of the individuals of the society. Acts promotive of the general welfare are good, welfare-retarding ones are bad—and that's that. It is all a question of effects, and the ways and means by which these effects are brought about do not enter in. At precisely this point the strictly ethical merit of the position is very vulnerable. Its weakness comes to light through the old dialectic of ends and means,

---

5. "Generally speaking" is not a pointless hedge. In the arbitration at issue, the arbiter generally dealt with *given* utilities. At present, however, he is entitled to *transform* them (on such grounds as discounting *Schadenfreude*). For example, suppose he contemplates the following distribution of first-order utility:

	I	II
A	+ 9	+10
B	+10	+ 9

Now if A is disposed toward B in an affectively positive manner (say at 30%) while B is *neutral* toward A, these distributions will have the following second-level aspect:

	I	II
A	+13	+12.7
B	+10	+ 9

On this basis, alternative I is clearly preferable.

But now suppose this distribution was to be made not just once or twice but very frequently. It seems reasonable that here, too, the arbiter should discount the operation of the vicarious affects in some suitable way, and should not allow A to become the *permanent* victim of his unreciprocated affection for B.

which merits acknowledgment and respect in this context. For an important point is brought home by the examples we have adduced in relation to the negative affects, which—as we have seen—may well work out in a happiness-augmenting way but, nevertheless, are ethically invalid. What counts from the viewpoint of ethical legitimation is not just *that* people are happier (in a better condition in point of welfare or utility) but *how* they get that way—whether by morally healthy and ethically legitimate means (such as sympathy) or by morally reprehensible and ethically illegitimate means (such as a perverse *Schadenfreude*).

It *is not morally defensible* to adopt happiness maximization as the standard when the vicarious affects are taken into account. Consider again the case[6] of two alternatives for a micro-society of five individuals (*A* to *E*) who are mutually inclined in an antipathetic manner (at a p.t.r. of −30 percent), two alternative distributions of utility being at issue:

	Alternative I	Alternative II
A	+10	−10
B	+10	−10
C	+10	−10
D	+10	−10
E	+10	−10

When the vicarious affects are taken into account, these distributions are transformed into

	I	II
A	−2	+2
B	−2	+2
C	−2	+2
D	−2	+2
E	−2	+2

Unhappily, the second allocation is emphatically preferable. Envy alone will translate an objective improvement in everyone's condition into a general detriment. But this, as we have contended,

6. See p. 82.

does not deserve *moral* recognition.[7] In a highly envious society, a step that best advances the happiness of all need not be morally right.

The essentially negative role of envy in establishing a *de facto* preference for a certain alternative may make this preference unworthy of *de jure* recognition. The first-order welfare of people provides a basis for the social recognition of claims that their second-order welfare does not *automatically* match. The dialectic of means and ends has a profound bearing upon this question of social legitimation, and where the mechanisms of affection come into play in a negative way (through envy, *Schadenfreude*, or the like), there is no reason to take the view that their influence deserves to be reckoned in the scale of social valuation.

The negative vicarious affects illustrate the important line of distinction between the preferences of a social group and its actual *welfare* in the standard sense of its *objective* condition in point of well-being.

From this standpoint, the tendency among economists to interpret welfare in terms of preference is put in a clear but damaging light. Anyone who is concerned for the social good of a group in any objective and meaningful sense has to realize (as parents, physicians, attorneys, and social workers generally do) that there may be a wide gap between what an individual prefers and what redounds to his genuine welfare and valid interests. The welfare or well-being of people is an objective condition that cannot be extracted from anything as tenuous and volatile as their preferences. The economists' penchant for deriving group welfare from considerations of personal preference

7. It is not the task of this short book to develop an overall moral theory rival to the utilitarian approach we criticize. Nor, indeed, is a full-dress moral theory requisite to our purposes. All that is essential for our needs is the concession of four or five moral theses in the area of common ground shared by commonsense morality and by some major sectors of philosophical tradition. These theses may thus be taken as sufficiently firm in their grounding to tilt the presumption of acceptability against any doctrine or theory that stands in conflict. Thus, while I do indeed espouse a rival ethical theory (one that deploys a complex combination of intuitivist, pragmatist, and idealistic ideas), there is no need to invoke this theory here. For there is nothing in the present critique of utilitarianism that hinges delicately on any of the details of this specific rival theory, as contradistinguished from a wide spectrum of other theoretical or commonsensical positions.

requires the working of a "hidden hand" to assure that the personal preferences at issue have any real bearing upon the actual *welfare* of the group, and this is a *deus ex machina* whose postulation is far from realistic.[8]

Of course, drawing this distinction among a man's utility-interests—between those that merit merely *de facto* recognition and those that merit recognition *de jure*, between those that deserve an "ideal observer's" recognition and those that do not—has drastic implications for the viability of utilitarianism. For the orthodox utilitarian must take his utilities as he finds them; he is not free to admit some and dismiss others on the basis of considerations that are, in the final analysis, *moral*. On a utilitarian approach, normative considerations must *reflect* considerations of utility and cannot modify or *transform* them. We shall return to this crucial issue in the final section of this chapter.

THE DEFECTS OF UTILITARIAN INDIVIDUALISM

Traditional utilitarianism treats social utility as the mere sum or aggregate of individual utilities. This approach is absolutely fundamental to its vision of society as a group of individuals that is without any collective interests or concerns of its own, over and above the distributive condition in the "utility" of its members. On this approach, it is crucial that the utilities of individuals be treated as sovereign, above and beyond criticism from the social point of view, since it is they who provide the determinative inputs that define just what the social point of view is to be. The definitive central doctrine of utilitarianism is that the *social* merit of a policy—or another measure that results in some distribution of "utility" (that is, good things and bad)—is to be assessed purely in terms of its favorable and unfavorable effects *on individuals*, and that this issue of individual impact is to be the *sole* standard of social merit.[9]

---

8. For a further critique of the move from preference to welfare see "A Critique of Welfare Economics" in N. Rescher, *Essays in Philosophical Analysis* (Pittsburgh, 1969).

9. From the standpoint of this *fundamental* commitment, the specific *mode* of determination for assessing the relative social merit of various individual distributions (greatest *average* utility, greatest *total* utility, greatest *minimal* utility for the most poorly rewarded, etc.) remains a secondary issue.

The pattern of individual-pertaining goods and evils is to be wholly determinative; the social good is determined through these alone, without alteration or amendment. Individual utilities must, therefore, be taken at face value: we must not, according to utilitarian theory, look into the mouth of the gift horse to reevaluate utility from some transcendent "social point of view." From the social standpoint of utilitarianism, individual utilities are sacred: *they are unalterable givens that are collectively determinative of the social good.*

This fundament of utilitarian theory encounters serious difficulty from the vicarious affects. The question becomes crucial: In assessing the "utility" that accrues to an individual in some circumstance, are we or are we not to take the vicarious affects into account? No matter how we turn here, we encounter serious difficulty; it is a matter of "damned if you do and damned if you don't."

If we refuse to take account of the vicarious affects, we meet the complaint: "How can you decline to recognize the pleasure (or displeasure) a man derives from the good fortune (or ill fortune) of his connections (family, friends, colleagues, etc.)? The pleasure (or pain) a person obtains in this way is every bit as real as that which he derives from developments that affect him personally. Nay—a parent may well feel his child's successes and failures every bit as acutely as his own."

On the other hand, if we admit the subsumption of the vicarious affects into the determination of personal utilities, someone will quite properly object as follows: "Suppose people in general were rather envious in a society. The goods of others substantially detract from their own. Then what appears in the first instance as a gain in everyone's welfare may well turn out to be a diminution thereof once the vicarious affects are taken into account. But it is surely wrongheaded and wholly indefensible to let a 'real' gain in the general welfare be transmuted into a net loss by permitting envy (*ex hypothesi* improper and unjustified) to count against the worth of very real gains in the 'objective' general welfare."

Both these objections seem to me perfectly sound. Whether the utilitarian includes or excludes the vicarious affects in assessing the utility-status of individuals, there arise serious difficulties *vis-à-vis* the moral defensibility of the resulting theory.

The only way out of the difficulty is one that is not available to the utilitarian, namely, to admit *some* vicarious affects into the social calculation and to exclude others—in short, to set up moral criteria as an arbiter over the points of view of individuals, and to let social standards function to allow or disallow individual claims.

Utilitarians (and the economists who are their spiritual heirs) want to maximize utility (satisfactions)—period. Nothing is said about maximizing good utility or maximizing utility in a good rather than bad way. Indeed, the whole idea of differentiating between the good and the bad with respect to utility itself is ideologically unwelcome to the utilitarians—a fact rather illustrated than refuted by J. S. Mill's struggles with just this problem. On the utilitarian approach, the very distinction between good and bad should be seen as the emergent result of an analysis of utility-implications. The idea that a distinction between ethical goods and evils, rather than being a *product* of utilitarian analysis, must be an *input* into it, crucially violates the very spirit of the utilitarian enterprise. Yet from the moral point of view, the critical evaluation of means is not only feasible but necessary. The fact that utilitarian theory not only *fails* to envisage the evaluative prospect, but decisively *precludes* it, is a substantial deficiency.

Yet to take such a utility-evaluative approach—which a reckoning with the vicarious affects shows to be necessary—is to recognize the untenability of utilitarianism at a point that lies close to the very core of the enterprise. For it points toward a view of the relationship between individual and social utility that is not one of unidirectional determination but of reciprocity and mutual influence. On the orthodox utilitarian view, utility is an inherently *individualistic* concept. Every man is an island whose utilities are determined in isolation, without reference to how others are faring. This overlooks the fact that when such distributions occur, the vicarious affects come into operation in such a way that utilities not only play the role of inputs but to some extent figure as outputs as well. But once one departs from the unrealism at issue, some of the cherished central dogmas of orthodox utilitarian theory are seriously impaired.

The very core of utilitarian theory is that morality is to be derived from group utility, and group utility is to be determined in terms of the utility of individuals. Thus the utilitarian must avoid—at the peril of vicious circularity for his whole enterprise—letting moral considerations enter into a determination of the utilities of individuals.

THE SOCIAL ASPECT

A process of evaluating the utilities of individuals in terms of their social implications goes dead against the utilitarian grain. For then the interests of the community are not simply a matter of the uncriticized satisfaction of its constituent individuals. Communal interest now becomes—nonreductivistically—a question of the need of a society to define its own holistic and larger-interests-oriented standard to override and control the aggregative interests of its constituent members. The social point of view comes to be the arbiter, discounting or emphasizing personal utilities in the light of socially oriented evaluative standards. The values and ideals of the group as a holistic unit (rather than simply an "additive aggregate" of individuals) come to play the crucial role in the framework of rational evaluation. From the social point of view, one must therefore discount or discountenance certain individual utilities, according to their nature. One cannot just ask "Does it produce satisfaction?" but must also inquire "*How* does it produce satisfaction?" (For example, pleasure at the pleasures of the wicked is not automatically to be taken at its hedonic face value. From the moral angle, the question of the *appropriateness* of vicarious affects cannot be ignored.) There can be no doubt that in any adequate reckoning on the scale of social recognition one must view the positive and the negative vicarious affects in a very different light: the former as generally deserving such recognition, the latter as crying out to be dismissed.

The upshot of this perspective is that one ceases to see satisfaction (happiness, utility, etc.) as an absolute good, but rather as an *end* in whose evaluation the traditional issue of *means* is still operative. Specifically, in the case of the negative affects we come to recognize that the well from which a quantity of utility is drawn can sometimes be poisoned. The vicarious affects play an important theoretical role in illustrating this crucial point: utility (happiness, satisfaction, etc.) is by no means of uniform status; it can be bad as well as good, deserving of dismissal as well as worthy of recognition.

To say this is not, of course, to deny that a doctrinaire and committed utilitarian cannot simply counter at this stage:

> Don't criticize the consequences of my theory because of
> conflicts with your putative "morality." All I care about—all
> that matters for me—is pleasure (or *utility*). I view your moral
> condemnation of its origins in certain cases (for example,
> *Schadenfreude*) as undeserving of serious consideration and
> altogether beside the point. I can attach no weight to any
> criticisms of my position on grounds of conflict with some
> self-styled "morality." The only morality worthy of the name
> is that which derives from utilitarian considerations, and *this*
> clearly cannot (*ex hypothesi*) conflict with the strictures of
> utilitarian theory.

But this stone-walling defense is an act of desperation. No
doubt, we cannot reason satisfactorily against any doctrinaire
adherent to a pet theory, *T*, who—whenever one adduces a
body of conflicting considerations, *C*—will blandly reply "Well,
so much the worse for *C*." We can never dissuade the fanatically
committed adherent to *T* if he is willing to go far enough down
this particular road. We can at best address ourselves to the
man who is sufficiently uncommitted to be able to grasp the
probative weight of contrary considerations without *parti pris*.
In developing a sufficiently weighty case we may not be able
to dissuade the totally committed doctrinaire, but we should
at least be able to prevent the as yet unpersuaded from becoming
committed in the first place.

The crucial factor, whose recognition is fatal to utilitarian
doctrine, is that it is necessary to distinguish between

1. *De facto* utilities, the utilities that people *actually* have,
   whose nature requires us to recognize the formative role
   of the negative vicarious affects, and
2. *De jure* utilities, the utilities that people *warrantedly* have
   (in the normative sense that they *deserve* to be recognized).
   Here we are required to discount or disallow the operation
   of the negative vicarious affects.

This distinction is all-important from the standpoint of moral
philosophy, and (as we have seen) it cannot be drawn on utilitarian
grounds—since the discounting of the negative vicarious affects
cannot be motivated on the utilitarian ground of being in principle
conducive to promoting welfare (utility, happiness, etc.). The

vicarious affects thus serve to bring a fundamental flaw in utilitarian ethics into sharp relief.

Where orthodox utilitarianism sees a unidirectional determination of social utilities in terms of personal ones, any ultimately tenable theory must reckon with a reciprocal influence process based on mutual feedback. To be sure, the utilities of individuals must play an important part in the determination of social utilities. But, inversely, social considerations will also condition, qualify, and (very possibly) *alter* those individual utilities which are to be allowed to enter into a social calculation.

The process of rational evaluation here at issue demands resort to considerations exterior to the utilitarian perspective. An evaluative assessment of the *means* by which such legitimate human ends as welfare (happiness, utility) are in fact realized requires the background of a larger vision of the ends of man. But developing the positive aspects of this perspective poses greater issues that go beyond the scope of this critique of utilitarianism. Suffice it to say that due heed of the implications of the vicarious affects of itself demonstrates the need for such a mechanism for the rational evaluation of human action, transcending the limited horizons of utilitarianism.[10]

Someone might be inclined to see an incongruity here, reasoning as follows:

> You maintain that utilitarianism cannot adequately come to terms with the vicarious affects. But you envisage no difficulties for the arbitrator's approach to the appraisal of people's interests in conflict-of-interest situations, as outlined in the preceding chapter. Now would it not be open to the utilitarian simply to adopt an arbitrative approach as a way of circumventing these difficulties?

The reply to this objection lies in noting just what the utilitarian would be committing himself to in this case. The "impartial arbiter" we have envisaged implements (*ex hypothesi*) an ap-

---

10. This issue of *de jure* and *de facto* utilities and the means used to achieve satisfaction poses difficulties for utilitarianism that are (in my view) independent of, and more fundamental than, the ramifications of first- and second-order utilities. (Thus the difficulties posed by *Schadenfreude* are in the final analysis, I suspect, really no different from those posed by ill-gotten utility gains of the first order.) But it does appear that the very nature of the affective process is such as to throw these difficulties into especially clear relief.

proach that does not take the "utilities" of the parties involved as sacrosanct and unquestionable givens, but merely as a starting point for critical assessment, introducing such distinctions as those between felt and real utilities, *de facto* and *de jure* utilities, and the like. Our arbiter, in short, does not proceed on utilitarian principles. In invoking *his* services, the utilitarian abandons the theoretical requirements of his own position.

The lesson at issue here goes beyond the confines of philosophical utilitarianism to touch upon the social sciences in general. For if the social scientist is not to confine himself to phenomenological description, but seeks to make the sort of normative evaluation that is indispensable to rational guidance with respect to programs and policies of action, the preceding considerations come to bear. For then one cannot proceed reductivistically and—by invoking utility or satisfaction or welfare or the like—attempt to avoid grappling with those fundamental issues of rational normative evaluation that form the staple concern of traditional moralists. In invoking utility or its congeners within the framework of his analysis, the social scientist cannot defensibly evade the need to define and delimit the role of ethical ideals in human affairs.

Recognition of the vicarious affects blocks the utilitarian vision of human action as the appropriate product of a calculation in which happiness, or satisfaction (or utility, etc.), is all. In the process of rational normative appraisal, one cannot avoid concern with the key issue of *how* this happiness comes to be constituted. This needed evaluation calls for the ethical appraisal of action to proceed not in terms of happiness production alone, but in terms of the realization of a substantially enlarged vision of the good for men. This important issue deserves a separate chapter.

6

~ The Social Rationale of Benevolence

The Gap Between Morality and Interest

Since the dawn of philosophical ethics in antiquity, some philosophers (at that early stage preeminently the Platonic Socrates and the Stoics) have sought the justification of morality in terms of personal advantage. It was argued that a man *should*—and, if rational, *will*—be moral on the strictly prudential grounds of true self-interest: one should be moral because it redounds to one's benefit to be. A simple formula captures the gist of this justificatory program: Why be moral?—because *it pays* to be so.

The only too evident and striking difficulties of this view—blazoned about us on every side by the all too frequently sorry condition of the good and thriving condition of the wicked—soon forced these theorists to take the primrose path of maintaining a drastic distinction between the merely seeming or *apparent* interests of people, emplaced on the surface, and their true or *genuine* interests, which lie beyond the scrutiny of the common gaze. The inherent problems and paradoxes of this position are so formidable that this line of defense represents a virtually forlorn hope—short of the blatant cheat of twisting the sense of "true interest" so as to encompass "being moral" within its meaning.

One may as well face the fact that the gap between prudential self-interest and morality cannot be closed by any amount of twisting and turning at the level of theoretical argumentation. Convincing examples are readily constructed—we have noted several of them in these pages—to show that action taken on the basis of prudential self-interest need not conduce to furthering the general good, supposing for the moment that such furtherance is what the dictates of morality demand in the case at hand. It is only too obvious that actions that serve one's own interest need not promote—and may indeed seriously injure—the interests of others. As the preceding deliberations have maintained time and again, one cannot derive morality from prudence by showing that doing the morally requisite thing will inevitably, or preponderantly, pay off in terms of personal advantage.

Still, might it not be possible to establish that the very prudence of the self-orientedly prudent man will lead him toward working for a moral order in which he and others are alike committed to acting morally? The argument at issue may be indicated by the following sketch of how—so it is maintained—the prudent man is bound to reason:

Since the selfishly prudent man will wish—merely on prudential grounds—to live in the midst of a suitably moral order, he cannot avoid the circumstance that other people will have certain expectations about him, and will make certain demands upon him as regards a commitment to morality—expectations to which they will give effective expression in the choice of political leadership, in education, in the formation of public institutions, etc. But other things being anything like equal, it is rational to espouse the bringing about of circumstances where certain demands can validly and reasonably be made upon oneself only if one is prepared to meet these demands. (It would be unreasonable—even foolish—of me to promote the creation of demands upon me that I feel constrained to reject.) Accordingly, the (prudentially motivated) desideratum of living in the midst of a moral order carries with it, by way of "consistency," an implicit rational commitment to the acceptance of this order—that is, to a part of it.

But this line of argument is ultimately unsatisfactory. For a rigoristically prudential man would certainly not be deterred by the merely *qualitative* anomaly of creating demands upon himself that he is unwilling to meet; rather, he would insist on weighing *the magnitude of the disadvantages* that would result. And these would very likely be minimal. Since he would in general *act* morally (on prudential grounds), his failure would be one of motivation, and would lie secure in the privacy of his internal forum. The overt damage caused by his putative "inconsistency" is thus minimized—and indeed more than offset by the presumptive advantage of his living in the midst of a moral order he is in a position to take advantage of through occasional acts of selfishness. Thus the indicated reduction cannot attain its goals: twist and turn it as one will, one cannot reshape morality into the prudence of self-interest.

MORALITY AND THE VICARIOUS AFFECTS

It would, of course, be very convenient if something as inherently problematic and intractable as moral theory could be extracted from something as relatively straightforward as human satisfaction. After considering the disagreements of opinion among moral theorists and the divergences of practice between the moral codes of different individuals and peoples, one turns with a sigh of relief to the relative straightforwardness of the *satisfactions* of man (his welfare, happiness, utility, or whatever).

Unfortunately, however, the simplification will not work. Morality cannot rest at the limits of what is, in the final analysis, an individual's private standpoint; it must adopt and implement the social point of view, and must do this in such a way that each individual's satisfactions and dissatisfactions are evaluated by a process from which moral considerations cannot be excluded. It is pointless to attempt a rational evaluation of human action if one is not willing to engage in considerations of positive morality. The rationality of human agency and choice is inextricably bound up with moral considerations. For rationality is not just a matter of the limited assessment of the efficiency of means, but encompasses *their* inherent worthiness, as well as that of the ulterior ends toward which they conduce. And these issues have a moral aspect that can be neglected only at the cost of the viability of the evaluative enterprise.

These considerations present a crucial part of the ethical rationale of the vicarious affects, for someone might well attempt to argue as follows:

In maintaining the moral legitimacy of the vicarious affects you have ignored the larger social picture. Thus, for example, vicarious affects based on *existing* relations in an unjust society could increase injustice, not right it. Internalization may work against social justice when the underdogs are moved to take pride in the successes of their more fortunate compeers, while the privileged neglect a reciprocal internalization (or internalize only the fate of their fellows in privilege). Only when one is sure that affective kinships reflect a justly organized system of relationships can one feel confident that community loyalty and love of kin will promote justice.

All this is true enough. There can be no abstract guarantee on grounds of theoretical principle that the vicarious affects must work in favor of socially desirable ends. The vicarious affects are, after all, simply one of the many facets of a person's utilities. And our critique of utilitarianism has insisted that utilities not be treated as sacred—that, indeed, the rational reassessment of personal utilities in the light of the wider interests of the common good is morally necessary and desirable. One must recognize and concede the fact that the preceding defense of the ethical legitimacy of the vicarious affects makes no pretense to establish them as ultimate, wholly sacrosanct, and totally indefeasible. We have merely insisted that they have a properly weighty role in ethical deliberation, not that they are pivots around which all else must be made to revolve. (At this juncture our invocation of the impartial arbiter becomes significant. His *ratio essendi*, after all, is to determine the just place of the separate utility-concerns of atomistic individuals in the overall social scheme of evaluation. And this mandate enables him to serve as a link between synoptic social concerns such as justice on the one hand and, on the other, the idiosyncratically diversified proliferation of personal utilities, specifically including those arrived at through the operation of the vicarious affects.)

It is instructive to consider in this light Kant's dictum that "a duty is a constraint to an end that is not gladly adopted."[1] This overlooks two important (and interrelated) considerations. The first is Aristotle's insistence that it is, after all, a central task of moral education to induce people to take pleasure in doing their duty, or at any rate to make this a point of pride and satisfaction. The second is the pivotal point that it is a

---

1. *Metaphysical Principles of Virtue*, trans. T. Ellington (New York, 1964), p. 43.

task of moral agency to create circumstances in which doing one's duty is transformed, insofar as possible, into a matter of self-interest by way of social sanctions and rewards. In the light of these considerations, rigid opposition between dutiful conscientiousness and personal satisfaction becomes untenable.

This perspective highlights the moral role of the vicarious affects. Internalization of the weal or woe of others obviously presents a way of narrowing the potential gap between morality and interest. Insofar as the welfare-status of others becomes part of our own (in the positive mode), the effect is that our own interest—thus amplified—comes to encompass the moral requisites of promoting the welfare of others. Vicarious participation makes the general good a component of our own and assimilates action in our enhanced self-interest to action in the public interest. Accordingly, the social imperative of fostering arrangements that coordinate personal advantage and the general interest calls for strengthening the operation of the vicarious affects. Their enhancement comes to be part of the morally requisite, albeit factually contingent, arrangements that are needed to close the gap between personal benefit and the public good.

The Conception of an "Adequate Moral Economy"

The thesis that if one acts so as to advance the general welfare of the social group, one thereby furthers one's personal welfare-interests is simply not a descriptive truth—it is not a statement of actual facts. But if the thesis of a reciprocal coordination of personal and social advantage is not an inescapable fact (and it is not), it is at any rate a regulative ideal. It is not actually so, but it *ought* to be. In an *ideal* state of affairs, it would surely be in the firsthand interest of people to promote the general good: someone who exerts himself for the welfare of his fellows ought not to find his own abridged thereby, and someone who consults his own best interests ought to find that in serving them he advances those of others as well.

This is indeed how things *ought* to be arranged, and how, in a morally well-ordered society, they actually *would* be. (To be sure nobody denies that this is *not* how they actually are.)

Thus we arrive at a socially oriented demand of individual morality, an injunction to act so as to realize a social order in which action for prudential advantage is—at least by and large—coincidental with action for the common good. From the moral point of view we ought to strive individually to realize a morally well-ordered society. And in a morally well-ordered society the correlation of action for individual advantage and for the social good *ought* to obtain; that is, the society ought to be so organized that this coordinative principle is operative.

We must recognize the social-engineering aspect of shaping a social order that has an "adequate moral economy" in this sense of coordination between action for both personal advantage and the general good. The circumstances of a society determine its desiderata of social-interaction situations—the customs and practices that make the channels of life flow smoothly (keeping an orderly queue versus a free-for-all, to take a very simpleminded example). The task is that of shaping a pattern of social incentives and sanctions (rewards and punishments) to assure balance between individual and general advantage by rendering socially benign action personally rewarding and antisocial action personally counterproductive. The development of institutions that both conduce toward socially advantageous and deter socially deleterious behavior is a crucial desideratum.

It merits stress that the nonutilitarian morality that underlies this position shares the characteristically attractive feature of utilitarian morality that sees moral obligation not simply in the negative terms of avoidance of wrongdoing (the essentially negative morality of the Old Testament injunction "Thou shalt not . . .") but as enjoining the creative effort needed to forge the conditions of an adequate moral economy. A properly ordered society has not only the *right* but the *duty* to foster a socially minded *modus operandi* by which its individuals are motivationally constrained to act for the common good.[2]

Thus while there is unquestionably a gap between individual and general advantage, there is a moral imperative to work toward narrowing it as much as possible, so as to create a public order that ensures an adequate moral economy: a coordination of

2. Of course, an "adequate moral economy" in which people will do the right thing, if only for prudential reasons of self-interest, is not yet a "morally superlative order" in which they do the right thing *for morally cogent reasons* (e.g., from a Kantian "sense of duty"). And, of course, we must recognize an obligation to work for *this* sort of system as well (by fostering moral education, etc.). But this (perfectly valid) point transcends the scope of our present concerns.

individual and social advantage within the framework of a calculus of interests. (Note that this coordination requires a social order in which people by and large are in a favorable condition of utility-endowment, for only then do the positive vicarious affects—which morality in principle enjoins upon us—produce prudential advantage.)

Consider three theses:

(1) It is (morally) incumbent on individuals to work for the realization of an adequate moral economy.

(2) It is personally advantageous that individuals have positive vicarious affects toward one another (to some extent) when they live in an adequate moral economy, and it is personally disadvantageous to have these affects in an economy of deprivation.

(3) It is in ordinary circumstances (morally) incumbent that individuals have positive vicarious affects toward one another (to some degree).

These premisses lead to the conclusion that

It is morally incumbent on individuals to work for the realization of a social order (namely, an adequate moral economy) within which that mutual sympathy—which it is morally incumbent upon them to exhibit—also turns out to be a matter of prudential advantage.

In sum, it emerges as a duty—albeit one seldom stressed by moralists—to work for a society in which both moral virtues and the virtuous themselves can thrive.

One must thus acknowledge the moral desideratum of forging an "adequate moral economy" that bridges the gap between actions conducive to prudential self-interest and those that further the general interest of the community. Clearly, however, the creation of such an economy as an aspect of the social organization of human interactions is beyond the capacities of the individual as an atomistically detached agent. (For just this reason we have characterized it as a *social* imperative that is more than a mere duty of individual morality.)

The dictates of morality demand that the private interest be harnessed to the general interest, so that the motive powers of individual action become productively conducive to the public weal. But the arrangements that can assure this linkage are not automatic, natural, and inevitable; they can only be a social creation, an *artifact*. Indeed, at the aggregative level needed to establish a moral economy, *only society* can foster the interests of the general good. The individual agent is impotent to do more than contribute his mite toward shifting society in this direction.

The circumstances of the case are such, however, that *the philosophers' penchant for connections of necessity is simply not operative*. The actual existence of a linkage between self-interested prudential advantage and the common good is a matter of the purely contingent and empirical circumstances of particular cases. Only if conditions happen to be appropriately arranged, through the creation of a social environment of a suitable sort, can there be proper coordination between these *in principle discordant* factors. (Though, to be sure, there lies in the background a moral imperative to realize a social order in which this linkage is operative.)

While it is morally incumbent upon individuals to work for the realization of an adequate moral economy, this need *not* be required of them on self-interested prudential grounds, in the sense of being an inevitable product of their intelligent pursuit of personal advantage. However, the contingent circumstances of the case may be such that this correlation in fact exists, and indeed (I have argued) it does so in the operative conditions of a modern advanced society. Of course, this hinges on a merely factual basis: it says nothing of the relationship of morality and self-interest at the level of theoretical principle. We have argued that no immediate relationship can be established here by abstract reasoning, and specifically that it cannot be demonstrated *in abstracto* to be in everyone's prudential interest to act morally.

Nonetheless, it can be maintained with reference to our conception of an adequate moral economy that it is in everyone's interest to create a social system in which it is in everyone's interest to act morally. This is so simply because the prevalence of a general moral order—a condition where people act morally by and large—is genuinely in the best interests of all concerned. Thus a relationship between interest and morality indeed exists, not at the first level but at the second remove: *Everyone has an interest that it be in everyone's interest to act as morality demands.*

Accordingly, the moralist should not condemn self-interest but should recognize a duty to ennoble it—a duty, that is, to foster circumstances in which selfish advantage is brought into coordination with the public interest, so that actions from these two very different ethical motivations should come to the same thing in practical effect.

THE HEGELIAN PERSPECTIVE

Insistence upon the moral legitimacy of the positive vicarious affects, in contradistinction to the negative ones, raises various questions. Above all, just *why* does this legitimacy obtain, given that it must surely be so not intrinsically, but for some further reason? This justificatory rationale is certainly not of utilitarian character—we have argued at length. What, then, is its nature?

We hold that the sought-for rationale is *Hegelian* in character. The credit of the positive and the discredit of the negative vicarious affects conduce to a social order that in turn is conducive to the capacity of individuals to lead *morally satisfactory* lives (in which they *have a right* to be satisfied) and to realize the full potential of human achievement in the creation of the social environment of human action. Considered in this way, the justificatory rationale at issue is no longer *utilitarian* (that is, predicated on happiness or welfare) but is still *instrumental*. It is a teleological matter of the arrangements facilitating a social order that is conducive to a certain *quality* of life (in the widest sense)—a life that people can lead in its social-interaction aspects with full rational contentment and without grounds for justified regrets about their actions and achievements.

One decisive difference between the present approach and that of utilitarianism deserves immediate notice. The utilitarian extracts private morality from the public good—for him, the morally right action is what best serves the general welfare. This quasi-totalitarian subordination of ethics to politics is definitely *not* part of the present program. On our approach, private morality is not a subordinate element of the general benefit but its autonomous, independent partner.

But there is another aspect of disagreement. Not only is our perspective counter to the utilitarian's totalitarian derivation of private morality from public interest, but it abandons his radically individualistic derivation of public interest from personal benefits. It joins the Hegelians of all persuasions who have always rejected the liberalistic dogma that the individuals who compose society, since it is their *interests* that are at stake, must be infallible judges of the social good. To the contrary, they regard questions of the social good as having an objective character that individuals can misperceive—individually or collectively—even as they can be mistaken about where their genuine interests lie.

Philosophers in the utilitarian tradition and their economist congeners espouse a theory of rationality in matters of social choice that proceeds in terms of an atomistic calculus of individual self-interests. This approach stands in marked contrast to the Hegelian tradition that contemplates a theory of rationality in sociocommunal terms, envisaging a pivotal role for certain irreducible (that is, not individualistically derivative) values. Such a holistic Hegelian approach to the concept of the common good stands in clear and direct opposition to a utilitarian, atomistic approach that tries to extract the good of all, wholly and entirely, from a separate consideration of the good of each. It is useful to view the deliberations of the present discussion against the background of this contrast in traditions.

The direction of thought developed here runs parallel with the Hegelian, societally contextual approach to morality, which is inherent in the idea that the social good of the group and the atomistic good of the individual agent are interlocked. For this is exactly the condition that obtains in what we have called an "adequate moral economy." And what is at issue is not just a facet of social morality but a point that penetrates into private morality through the personal duty to work toward the realization of a suitable moral order. Private morality is thus seen as *interdependent* with its social context—and indeed requires working for realization of a social context of a certain sort. We are led back to the Hegelian vision of a mutual dependence of the social and the personal—in that a morally optimal individual code of behavior is only realizable in, and must be correlated with, a benign social order.

THE IDEALISTIC ASPECT

For simplicity, let us coalesce all the felt satisfactions of life in the area of human well-being under the rubric of *welfare*. It must be stressed that this is an oversimplification; people may well take satisfaction (and quite legitimately) in actions or occurrences that—like Kantian works of duty—do not promote their "welfare" in any ordinary sense of that term. However, subject to this simplifying assumption, we may class the factors that augment the quality of life into two principal groups: the excellence-conducive and the welfare-conducive. The latter relate to objectives in the traditionally *pragmatic* range; the former are extrapragmatic, or, as we shall call them, *ideal* in nature. They relate to man's "higher" aspirations rather than to pleasure or satisfaction or happiness *per se*. Correspondingly, in assessing the quality of life we must operate with an essentially two-factor criterion in which both welfare and human excellence play a significant part.

That the quality of life cannot be assessed in terms of happiness, or even welfare alone, is an immediate implication of these rudimentary considerations. It is perfectly conceivable that one individual's personal happiness can be higher than another's (other things being equal), notwithstanding the former's lack of education, disinterest in culture and the arts, and disregard of the rights and interests of his fellows. But it would not follow that the individual who prospers in happiness or welfare is thereby superior in "quality of life." (We come back to the cutting edge of J. S. Mill's *obiter dictum:* "Better to be Socrates dissatisfied than a pig satisfied.")

Neither for individuals nor for societies is "the pursuit of happiness" the sole and legitimate guide to action; its dictates must be counterbalanced by recognizing the importance of doing those things upon which, in after years, we can look back with justifiable pride. No matter how we shape the details of our overarching vision of the good life for man, welfare will play only a partial and subsidiary role because a satisfactory condition of affairs *vis-à-vis* welfare is compatible with substantial impoverishment outside the sphere of welfare-related desiderata. Indeed a person, or a society, can be healthy, prosperous, and literate, but lack all those resources of personality, intellect, and character, such as cultivation of mind and human congeniality, that make life rewarding as well as pleasant. Toward people or nations that have—even to abundance—the constituents of welfare, we may well feel envy, but our *admiration* and *respect* could never be won on this ground alone. A vast dimension of legitimate human desiderata lies beyond welfare, indeed even beyond the realm of happiness as such.

The central concept of this excellence-connected, transwelfare domain is *quality*, particularly in the realization of human potentialities: in creativity, in the appreciation thereof, and in the forging of rewarding human interrelationships. Excellence, dignity, and the sense of worth are its leading themes. We have left behind the minima at issue with welfare to enter another sphere—that of human ideals relating to man's higher and nobler aspirations.

What justifies an insistence that society recognize the claims of excellence? Certainly not an appeal to social welfare—it smacks of brazen hypocrisy to argue that art galleries, or botanical gardens, theoretical physics, or the classical stage inevitably—somehow—advance the *welfare* of people. If the allocation of substantial social resources to museums, symphony orchestras, or institutes of advanced studies is justified—as I am convinced it is—this justification cannot proceed on the basis of welfare advancement. It should not proceed with reference to *welfare* at all (no matter how indirect) but, rather, in terms of something else just as important: *an investment in social ideals.* For the possession of ideals, values, and aspirations is patently a social desideratum *in its own right.* What is at issue here is not a practical, utilitarian defense in terms of welfare-benefits to people but an "idealistic" defense in terms of the general principle of human ideals.

The key point of these considerations for our present purposes lies in an analogy. Just as *individuals* have legitimate goals that transcend personal well-being to embrace the idea of *quality* of life in a broader, welfare-transcending sense, so societies have a holistic ideal of *the social good* which reaches beyond considerations of welfare to embrace those qualitative aspects of affairs relating to excellence in the realization of human potential. These welfare-transcending social goals are (1) not aggregative but holistic aspects of the social order as a unit (unlike social *welfare*, which tends—despite some difficulties—to be an aggregative function of the well-being of individuals), and are (2) related to the issue of quality or excellence rather than to those relating to well-being as such. Goals of this nature represent social *ideals* and definite rationally warranted *aspirations* for the realization of higher forms of social organization in the promulgation of cultural patterns, the structuring of social interaction, and the conduct of communal affairs.[3]

3. The issues of this section are treated at greater length in chap. 7 of the writer's *The Primacy of Practice* (Oxford, 1973), and the present discussion draws upon that chapter.

On this view, the tradition launched by Hegel in moral philosophy—however uncongenial to the contemporary atomistic-individualistic spirit—carries significant and useful lessons for our deliberations. The analysis points to a conception of the social good as holistic rather than derived from a quantitative compilation of individual goods. Hence, the weight given the individual goods in the moral calculation must itself be determined on the scale of social considerations (for example, by discarding those individual goods which—however real—must, like *Schadenfreude,* be denied any countenance on the basis of social considerations). To recognize a creature *as a person*—as a fellow human being with correlative rights and responsibilities—involves an act of idealization transcending any actual "evidence" we ever have in hand. It involves a transfactual imputation, made in the context of a moral theory, that constrains us to want certain things *of and for* him.[4]

Exactly the same is true with organized social groups: an adequate social theory will warrant our asking certain things of and for a society *as a society,* viewed collectively as an aggregate unit in its own right rather than distributively, relative to its component members. And the resultant symbiosis of levels makes it appropriate not only to criticize social concerns in the light of independently constituted individual interests, but also to criticize individual interests in the light of independently constituted social concerns. It is clear from this perspective that, notwithstanding its current, somewhat contemptuous neglect, the ethical doctrine of idealism contains ideas of substantial merit and usefulness in handling basic issues in contemporary ethical theory.

But we have come a long distance from our initial concern with the vicarious affects. In concluding, it is necessary to return to them.

CONCLUSION

The vicarious affects belong to what Adam Smith called "the *moral sentiments*"—those whose operation merit ethical approbation and whose widened role in human affairs it is a proper

---

4. For this imputational aspect see N. Rescher, *Conceptual Idealism* (Oxford, 1973), esp. pp. 180–83.

object of moral education to promote. They represent motives of action that men undoubtedly *do* widely exhibit and certainly *ought* to exhibit more widely. Thus on both factual grounds of *what is* the case and on normative grounds of *what ought to be* the case, there is no excuse for ignoring the workings of the vicarious affects among the operative forces of human affairs.

However, we have not maintained that, as the world actually turns, the vicarious affects by themselves play a decisive role in human affairs. To be sure, they play *some* role, and it can hardly be denied that this role will often prove important, particularly in the domestic orbit. Still, the role of the vicarious affects within the overall phenomenology of social interaction must not be exaggerated—as our intensive focus upon them may seem to have done. Their place is a *prominent* one, although by no means *predominant*.

Admittedly, the vicarious affects represent a small part of a complex landscape—small, but certainly not negligible. Though perhaps overly stressed by traditional moralists, they have, unfortunately, been largely ignored by modern economic and social theorists—to the marked detriment of their models of human motivation. For the penalties of this neglect are paid in significant deficiencies in such fields as the social theory of small-group interactions (for example, the family, the work environment), the economic theory of human motivation ("economic man" devoid of various "irrationalisms"), the utilitarian theory of ethics, and so on.

Thus despite the relatively modest role of the vicarious affects as a mode of motivation in human affairs, their *theoretical implications* are nevertheless strikingly significant. Like the *aqua regia* of little intrinsic value, which reveals the presence of true gold, the vicarious affects yield a yardstick by which to measure some of the strengths and deficiencies of various social theories. It is *this* service—not so much their *intrinsic* significance as their ability to provide a touchstone for the *systematic* adequacy of social theories and doctrines of moral philosophy—that I should like to leave in the reader's mind as a closing impression.

Bibliography
Name Index
Subject Index

Bibliography

Ethics and Moral Philosophy

Acton, H. B.
"The Ethical Importance of Sympathy." *Philosophy*, 30 (1955): 62-66.
Argues for an intimate relationship between morality and sympathy.
Baier, Kurt
The Moral Point of View. Ithaca, 1958.
See chap. 8 on egoism, as well as *passim*, for an acute discussion of relationships between morality and interest.
Bentham, Jeremy
An Introduction to the Principles of Morals and Legislation. London, 1789.
Deontology. Edited by John Bowring. Edinburgh and London, 1843.
Fragment on Government and Introduction to the Principles of Morals and Legislation. Edited by Wilfred Harrison. Oxford, 1948.
Braithwaite, R. B.
Theory of Games as a Tool for the Moral Philosopher. Cambridge, 1955.
Brandt, R. B.
Ethical Theory. Englewood Cliffs, N.J., 1958.
See chap. 14 on egoism.
Broad, C. D.
Five Types of Ethical Theory. London, 1930.
"Egoism as a Theory of Human Motives." In his *Ethics and the History of Philosophy.* London, 1952. Pp. 218-31.
Brunton, J. A.
"Egoism and Morality." *Philosophical Quarterly*, 6 (1956): 289-303.
Butler, Joseph
Fifteen Sermons upon Human Nature. London, 1726.
See esp. sermon 11, "Upon the Love of Our Neighbor."
Comte, Auguste
The Positive Philosophy of Auguste Compte. Edited by H. Martineau. 2 vols. London, 1853.
States a classic theory of social progress and the evolution of moral ideals in their social context.

Ewing, A. C.
    Ethics. London and New York, 1953.
    See esp. chap. 2, "Selfishness and Unselfishness."
Falk, W. D.
    "Morality, Self, and Others." In *Morality and the Language of Conduct.* Edited by Hector-Neri Castaneda and G. Nakhnikian. Detroit, 1965.
Frankena, William
    "Obligation and Motivation in Recent Moral Philosophy." In *Essays in Moral Philosophy.* Edited by A. I. Melden. Seattle, 1958.
Gauthier, D. P.
    Morality and Rational Self-Interest. Englewood Cliffs, N.J., 1970.
Hodgson, D. H.
    Consequences of Utilitarianism. London, 1967.
Hospers, John
    Human Conduct: An Introduction to the Problems of Ethics. New York, 1961.
Hume, David
    Essays: Moral, Political and Literary. Edinburgh, 1741.
    A Treatise of Human Nature. Edited by L. A. Selby-Bigge. Oxford, 1888.
    Enquiries Concerning the Human Understanding and Concerning the Principles of Morals. Edited by L. A. Selby-Bigge. 2d ed. Oxford, 1902.
Hutcheson, Francis
    An Enquiry Concerning Moral Good and Evil. London, 1729.
    A System of Moral Philosophy. London, 1755.
James, William
    Psychology. New York, 1892.
    "The Moral Philosopher and the Moral Life." In *The Will to Believe.* New York, 1897.
Kant, Immanuel
    Groundwork of the Metaphysic of Morals. Trans. by H. J. Paton. London, 1948.
Kaufmann, Henry
    Aggression and Altruism. New York, 1970.
Körner, Stephan, ed.
    Practical Reason. Oxford, 1974.
Maclagan, W. G.
    "Self and Others: A Defense of Altruism." *Philosophical Quarterly,* 4 (1954): 109-27.
    "Respect for Persons as a Moral Principle." *Philosophy,* 35 (1960): 193-305.
Mandeville, Bernard

Fables of the Bees. London, 1705.
McCloskey, H. J.
  Meta-Ethics and Normative Ethics. The Hague, 1969.
Medlin, Brian
  "Ultimate Principles and Ethical Egoism." *Australasian Journal of Philosophy,* 35 (1957): 111–18.
Mercer, Philip
  Sympathy and Ethics. London, 1972.
  A study of the role of sympathy in Hume's moral philosophy. Chap. 1 ("The Logic of Sympathy") and chap. 7 ("Sympathy as a Precondition of Morality") are of independent value.
Mill, John Stuart
  Utilitarianism. London, 1863.
Moore, G. E.
  Principia Ethica. Cambridge, 1903.
Nagel, Thomas
  The Possibility of Altruism. Oxford, 1970.
Narveson, Jan
  Morality and Utility. Baltimore, 1967.
  An Acute and dogged defense of utilitarian morality.
Nielsen, Kai
  "Egoism in Ethics." *Philosophy and Phenomenological Research,* 19 (1959): 502–10.
Prichard, H. A.
  Duty and Interest. Oxford, 1928.
  Moral Obligations. Oxford, 1949.
Rand, Ayn
  The Virtue of Selfishness. 2d ed. New York, 1964.
  See esp. chaps. 1 and 5.
Rashdall, Hastings
  The Theory of Good and Evil. 8 vols. Oxford, 1924.
Rawls, John
  A Theory of Justice. Cambridge, Mass., 1972.
Reiner, Hans
  Pflicht und Neigung. Meisenheim am Glan, 1951.
Rescher, Nicholas
  Distributive Justice. New York, 1966.
Rutherford, Thomas
  Essay on the Nature and Obligations of Virtue. Cambridge, 1744.
Scheler, Max
  The Nature of Sympathy. Trans. by P. L. Heath. London, 1954.
Schlick, Moritz
  Problems of Ethics. Trans. by D. Rynin. New York, 1939.
  See chaps. 2 and 3 on egoism.

Schoeck, Helmut
   Envy: A Theory of Social Behavior. Trans. by M. Glemmy and
   B. Ross. New York, 1970.
Schopenhauer, Arthur
   On the Basis of Morality. Trans. by A. B. Ballock. London, 1903.
   Also trans. by E. F. J. Payne. New York, 1965.
Schwarzman, K. A.
   *Ethik ohne Moral: Kritik der modernen bürgerlichen ethischen
   Theorien.* Berlin, 1967.
Scott-McTaggart, M. J.
   "Butler on Disinterested Actions." *Philosophical Quarterly,* 18 (1968):
   16–28.
Shaftesbury, A. A. C.
   Enquiry Concerning Virtue. London, 1699.
Sidgwick, Henry
   The Methods of Ethics. London, 1874; 7th (last) ed. London, 1907.
   For egoism see chap. 7 of bks. I and II; for benevolence see
   chap. 4 of bk. III.
Smith, Adam
   The Theory of Moral Sentiments. London, 1759.
   See esp. the discussion of sympathy in sec. I of pt. I.
Spencer, Herbert
   Data of Ethics. London, 1879.
   See esp. chaps. 11 and 12 on egoism and altruism.
   Principles of Ethics. London, 1892.
   See esp. chap. 4 of pt. IV.
Spinoza, Benedict
   Ethics. London, 1910.
   See esp. bk. III.
Stace, W. T.
   The Concept of Morals. New York, 1937.
   See esp. chap. 9, "Morals and Motives."
Wand, Bernard
   "A Note on Sympathy in Hume's Moral Theory." *Philosophical
   Review,* 64 (1955): 275–79.

PSYCHOLOGY

Aronfreed, Justin
   "The Origins of Altruistic and Sympathetic Behavior." Paper present-
   ed in symposium on altruism at annual meeting of American
   Psychological Association, 1966.
   *Conduct and Conscience: The Socialization of Internalized Control
   Over Behavior.* New York, 1968.

Surveys the psychological literature of internalization.
"The Concept of Internalization." In *Handbook of Socialization Theory and Research.* Edited by D. A. Goslin. Chicago, 1969.

Bain, Alexander
The Emotions and the Will. London, 1859.

Berger, S. M.
"Conditioning Through Vicarious Instigation." *Psychological Review,* 69 (1962): 450-66.

Campbell, D. T.
"Ethnocentric and Other Altruistic Motives." In *Nebraska Symposium on Motivation.* Edited by D. Levine. Lincoln, 1965. Pp. 283-311.

James, William
Psychology. 2 vols. New York, 1891-92.

Kohlberg, Lawrence
Stages in the Development of Moral Thought and Action. New York, 1971.

Krebs, D. L.
"Altruism: An Examination of the Concept and a Review of the Literature." *Psychological Bulletin,* 73 (1970): 258-302.

Lewis, D. J., and Duncan, C. P.
"Vicarious Experience and Partial Reinforcement." *Journal of Abnormal and Social Psychology,* 57 (1958): 321-26.

Macaulay, Jaqueline R., and Berkowitz, Leonard, eds.
Altruism and Helping Behavior. New York, 1970.
An interesting collection of empirical studies of psychological and sociological aspects. The chapter by Justin Aronfreed ("The Socialization of Altruistic and Sympathetic Behavior: Some Theoretical and Experimental Analyses") is of particular interest.

Masserman, J. H., Wechkin, S., and Terris, W.
"'Altruistic' Behavior in Rhesus Monkeys." *American Journal of Psychiatry,* 21 (1964): 584-85.

Shure, M. B.
"Fairness, Generosity, and Selfishness: The Naive Psychology of Children and Young Adults." *Child Development,* 39 (1968): 875-86.

SOCIOLOGY AND SOCIAL PSYCHOLOGY

Asch, S. E.
Social Psychology. New York, 1952.

Berkowitz, Leonard
"Responsibility, Reciprocity and Social Distance in Help-Giving: An Experimental Investigation of English Social Class Difference." *Journal of Experimental Social Psychology,* 4 (1968): 46-63.

Budd, L. J.
    "Altruism Arrives in America." *American Quarterly*, 8 (1956): 40-52.
Friedrichs, R. W.
    "Alter Versus Ego: An Exploratory Assessment of Altruism." *American Sociological Review*, 25 (1960): 496-508.
    A report on the empirical data of a questionnaire study.
Gallo, P. S., and McClintock, C. G.
    "Cooperative and Competitive Behavior in Mixed Motive Games." *Journal of Conflict Resolution*, 9 (1965): 68-78.
Harris, L. A.
    "A Study of Altruism." *Elementary School Journal*, 68 (1967): 135-41.
Homans, G. C.
    Social Behavior: Its Elementary Forms. New York, 1961.
Kropotkin, Pëtr Alekseevich
    Mutual Aid: A Factor of Evolution. London, 1902.
    A study of the pattern of action whose springs guide a man to act (as the conclusion puts it) "not merely by love, which is always personal, or at best tribal, but by the perception of his oneness with each human being."
Leeds, Ruth
    "Altruism and the Norm of Giving." *Merrill-Palmer Qualterly*, 9 (1963): 229-40.
Lerner, M. J., and Lichtman, R. R.
    "Effects of Perceived Norms on Attitudes and Altruistic Behavior Toward A Dependent Other." *Journal of Personality and Social Psychology*, 9 (1968): 226-232.
Luce, R. D., and Raiffa, Howard
    Games and Decisions: Introduction and Critical Survey. New York, 1957.
Macaulay, Jaqueline R., and Berkowitz, Leonard, eds.
    Altruism and Helping Behavior. New York, 1970.
    An interesting collection of empirical studies of psychological and sociological aspects. The chapter by Justin Aronfreed ("The Socialization of Altruistic and Sympathetic Behavior: Some Theoretical and Experimental Analyses") is of particular interest.
Midlarsky, Elizabeth
    "Aiding Responses: An Analysis and a Review." *Merrill-Palmer Quarterly*, 14 (1968): 229-60.
Murphy, L. B.
    Social Behavior and Child Personality: An Exploratory Study of Some Roots of Sympathy. New York, 1937.
Ribal, J. E.
    "Social Character and Meanings of Selfishness and Altruism." *Sociology and Social Research*, 47 (1963): 311-21.

Sawyer, Jack
  "The Altruism Scale." *American Journal of Sociology,* 71 (1966): 407-16.
Simmons, C. H., and Lerner, M. J.
  "Altruism as a Search for Justice." *Journal of Personality and Social Psychology,* 9 (1968): 216-25.
Solomon, Leonard
  "The Influence of Some Types of Power Relationships and Game Strategies upon the Development of Interpersonal Trust." *Journal of Abnormal and Social Psychology,* 61 (1960): 223-30.
Sorokin, P. A.
  Altruistic Love. Boston, 1950.
Sorokin, P. A., ed.
  Explorations in Altruistic Love and Behavior. Boston, 1952.
  Forms and Techniques of Altruistic and Spiritual Growth. Boston, 1954.
Turner, W. C.
  "Altruism and Its Measurement in Children." *Journal of Abnormal and Social Psychology,* 43 (1948): 502-16.
Wright, B. A.
  "Altruism in Children and the Perceived Conduct of Others." *Journal of Abnormal and Social Psychology,* 37 (1942): 218-33.
Wright, Derek
  The Psychology of Moral Behavior. Baltimore, 1971.

Economics

Arrow, K. J.
  Social Choice and Individual Values. New York, 1963.
Goldstick, Daniel
  "Assessing Utilities." *Mind,* 80 (1971): 531-41.
Körner, Stephan, ed.
  Practical Reason. Oxford, 1974.
Marschak, Jacob
  "Rational Behavior, Uncertain Prospects, and Measurable Utility." *Econometrica,* 18 (1950): 111-41.
Rescher, Nicholas
  Distributive Justice. New York, 1966.
Samuelson, P. A.
  Economics: An Introductory Analysis. 7th ed. New York, 1967.
Sen, A. K.
  Collective Choice and Social Welfare. San Francisco and London, 1970.

Smith, Adam
  The Theory of Moral Sentiments. London, 1759.
  See esp. the discussion of sympathy in sec. I of pt. I.

GAME AND DECISION THEORY

Arnaszus, Helmut
  Spieltheorie und Nutzenbegriff aus marxistischer Sicht. Frankfurt au
  Main, 1974.
Bixenstine, V. E., Potash, H. M., and Wilson, K. V.
  "Effects of Level of Cooperative Choice by the Other Player in
  Choices in a Prisoner's Dilemma Game: Part I." *Journal of Abnormal
  and Social Psychology,* 66 (1963): 308-13. Part II, *ibid.,* 67 (1963):
  134-147.
Braithwaite, R. B.
  Theory of Games as a Tool for the Moral Philosopher. Cambridge,
  1955.
David, Morton D.
  Game Theory. New York, 1970.
Gallo, P. S., and McClintock, C. G.
  "Cooperative and Competitive Behavior in Mixed Motive Games."
  Journal of Conflict Resolution, 9 (1965): 68-78.
Klaus, Georg
  Spieltheorie in philosophischer Sicht. Berlin, 1968.
Luce, R. D., and Raiffa, Howard
  Games and Decisions: Introduction and Critical Survey. New York,
  1957.
Raiffa, Howard
  "Arbitration Schemes for Generalized Two-Person Games." In *Con-
  tributions to the Theory of Games.* Edited by H. W. Kuhn and
  A. W. Tucker. Princeton, 1953, pp. 361 ff.
Rapoport, Anatol
  Strategy and Conscience. New York, 1964.
  Two-Person Game Theory: The Essential Ideas. Ann Arbor, 1966.
  "Escape from Paradox." *Scientific American,* 217 (1967): 50-56.
Rapoport, Anatol, and Chammah, Albert
  Prisoner's Dilemma: A Study in Conflict and Cooperation. Ann Arbor,
  1965.
Schelling, Thomas C.
  The Strategy of Conflict. Cambridge, Mass., 1960.
  "Experimental Games and Bargaining Theory." In *The International
  System.* Edited by K. Knorr and S. Verba. Princeton, 1961. Pp.
  47-68.

Sen, A. K.
  Collective Choice and Social Welfare. San Francisco and London, 1970.
Solomon, Leonard
  "The Influence of Some Types of Power Relationships and Game Strategies upon the Development of Interpersonal Trust." *Journal of Abnormal and Social Psychology,* 61 (1960): 223-30.

Name Index

Subject Index